Adam Smith: A Very Short Introduction

VERY SHORT INTRODUCTIONS are for anyone wanting a stimulating and accessible way into a new subject. They are written by experts, and have been translated into more than 45 different languages.

The series began in 1995, and now covers a wide variety of topics in every discipline. The VSI library currently contains over 550 volumes—a Very Short Introduction to everything from Psychology and Philosophy of Science to American History and Relativity—and continues to grow in every subject area.

Very Short Introductions available now:

Available soon:

MODERN ARCHITECTURE
  Adam Sharr
BIOMETRICS
  Michael Fairhurst

GLACIATION David J. A. Evans
TYPOGRAPHY Paul Luna
ENVIRONMENTAL ETHICS
  Robin Attfield

For more information visit our website

www.oup.com/vsi/

Christopher J. Berry

ADAM SMITH

A Very Short Introduction

OXFORD
UNIVERSITY PRESS

OXFORD
UNIVERSITY PRESS

Great Clarendon Street, Oxford, OX2 6DP,
United Kingdom

Oxford University Press is a department of the University of Oxford.
It furthers the University's objective of excellence in research, scholarship,
and education by publishing worldwide. Oxford is a registered trade mark of
Oxford University Press in the UK and in certain other countries

Published in the United States of America by Oxford University Press
198 Madison Avenue, New York, NY 10016, United States of America

British Library Cataloguing in Publication Data

Data available

Library of Congress Control Number: 2018945262

ISBN 978-0-19-878445-6

Printed in Great Britain by
Ashford Colour Press Ltd, Gosport, Hampshire

Contents

Contents

Acknowledgements

My thanks to Adrian Birchall for recurrently playing the role of 'target reader'; his responses have greatly helped as I shaped my text. I have occasionally imposed on members of my family (especially 'the other Chris') for feedback on style, wording, and 'sense' for which I both apologize and express my gratitude. I do, of course, owe a generalized debt to the community of Smith scholars but, more specifically, to Craig Smith for his input on Chapter 7. Finally I thank Andrea Keegan for inviting me to write this book and Jenny Nugee for her support thereafter. It has been an enjoyable challenge.

List of illustrations

Abbreviations

I insert into the text the following abbreviations followed by page number; these all refer to the Glasgow Edition of Smith's Works, published by the Liberty Press, Indianapolis.

CL	'Considerations concerning the First Formation of Languages', in *LRBL*
Corr	*Correspondence of Adam Smith*, E. Mossner and I. Ross (eds) (1987)
EPS	*Essays on Philosophical Subjects*, W. Wightman (ed.) (1982)
HA	'The Principles which lead and direct Philosophical Enquiries illustrated by the History of Astronomy', in *EPS*
IA	'Of the Imitative Arts', in *EPS*
Life	*Account of the Life and Writings of Adam Smith*, by Dugald Stewart, in *EPS*
LJ	*Lectures on Jurisprudence*, R. Meek, D. Raphael, and P. Stein (eds) (1982)
LRBL	*Lectures on Rhetoric and Belles-Lettres*, J. Bryce (ed.) (1985)
TMS	*The Theory of Moral Sentiments*, A. Macfie and D. Raphael (eds) (1982)
WN	*An Inquiry into the Nature and Causes of the Wealth of Nations*, R. Campbell and A. Skinner (eds) (1981)

The Author of the Wealth of Nations

1. Engraving of Adam Smith (1790) by John Kay.

Chapter 1
Life and times

Adam Smith is the author of the *Wealth of Nations*, one of the
great works in the history of economics. But it is little read, even
by economists who are content to pay lip-service to him as a
'founding father' of their discipline. On a broader front his name
conjures up the promotion of self-interest and opposition to the
state interfering in the market-place, which together will produce
prosperity and liberty. For some this is a positive image, Smith's
principles lay the foundation for individual and social well-being.
For others the picture is negative, Smith's principles lie at the
heart of social inequality and individual exploitation. But both of
these are gross over-simplifications. For one thing the *Wealth of
Nations* is a large, complex book that cannot be reduced to a
snappy summary. There is also much more to Smith than a book
on the workings of the economy. He wrote an important treatise
of moral philosophy, published an exceptionally well-informed
history of astronomy, and was an author who cared about literary
style and how to communicate both orally and in print.

Biographical outline

Adam Smith was born in 1723 in Kirkcaldy on the east coast
of Scotland. His father, also Adam, was a lawyer but he died
six months before his son was born. His mother (Margaret) never
re-married and Adam was a devoted son throughout her long

life—she only died in 1788 predeceasing him by just two years. Dugald Stewart, Smith's first biographer, who knew him and was able to gain additional information from contemporaries, remarks that Adam was a sickly child who received the loving care of his mother but who, in return, gratefully and dutifully repaid her affection over the course of her long life.

He attended the local school from about the age of 8 and benefited from the rigour and enthusiasm of a new master. Smith entered Glasgow University in 1737 at the early—but for the time not that unusual—age of 14. His school-gained proficiency in the classics was such that he was effectively able to by-pass the early years in the curriculum devoted to Latin and Greek. At Glasgow, Smith studied under some of the leading scholars of the day. His most important teacher was the Professor of Moral Philosophy, Francis Hutcheson. In a letter towards the end of his life, Smith paid eloquent tribute to Hutcheson's qualities as a teacher and as a philosopher, despite the fact that in his *Theory of Moral Sentiments* Smith openly disagreed with his views of benevolence and moral sense.

In 1740 Smith was awarded a Snell Scholarship (this is still in existence) to study at Balliol College, Oxford, where he stayed until 1746. This was not because he was enthralled by the education on offer; indeed in the *Wealth of Nations* he was scathing about the quality of the teaching and the teachers. He appears to have spent his time in private study. This, probably, included keeping up his scientific interests, cultivating his linguistic skills, and in developing, as Dugald Stewart conjectured, 'the study of human nature in all its branches, most particularly of the political history of mankind' (*Life* 271). At that time he almost certainly read David Hume's *A Treatise of Human Nature* (1739/40) and Hume was to become his closest friend.

On his return to Scotland in 1746 he went to live with his mother in Kirkcaldy but in 1748 he moved to Edinburgh where, thanks to the patronage of Henry Home—later ennobled as Lord Kames on his appointment as a judge—he was invited to give a series of lectures on rhetoric and later probably on law and philosophy. There is no record of the content of these lectures. They were well-received and he was asked to repeat them. Perhaps because of that success but also, crucially, with the support of Archibald Campbell, Earl of Ilay (later Duke of Argyll), Smith returned to Glasgow University as the Professor of Logic in 1751.

Argyll had a hand in many academic posts and he used his power of patronage to promote individuals who were disposed to modernizing Scottish society. There was one other candidate for the logic chair. Although the vote for Smith was unanimous, his rival (George Muirhead) was an able scholar, who later became Professor of Oriental Languages and then Humanity at Glasgow. In 1752 Smith was appointed, without competition, Professor of Moral Philosophy, a post he held for next twelve years until he left academic life.

Smith taught a wide variety of subjects. Besides courses in philosophy and jurisprudence he also lectured on history, literature, and language. A series of notes taken by students of his lectures on rhetoric and literature have been discovered and published as also have two sets of extensive student notes of his lectures on jurisprudence. Smith dictated his lectures so not only do these notes largely duplicate each other, they also give a reliable account of his subject-matter. In 1762 the university awarded him an LLD in virtue of his 'universally acknowledged reputation in letters and particularly that he has taught Jurisprudence these many years in this University with great applause.'

Smith published two great books and the seeds of both were sown in his Glasgow professorial years. The *Theory of Moral Sentiments* appeared in 1759 and went through six editions in his lifetime. The final one, containing extensive revisions, appeared in the year of his death (1790). These changes indicate that Smith's commitment to moral philosophy endured alongside and beyond the publication of the *Wealth of Nations*, his second great book published in 1776. Although by then Smith had left Glasgow, it is clear from the evidence of the student notes that he had already considered many of that book's leading themes, such as the division of labour, in his Glasgow classrooms. This judgment is backed up by the testimony of his pupil, later professorial colleague, John Millar who recalls that Smith lectured on 'those arts which contribute to subsistence, and to the accumulation of property, in producing correspondent movements or alterations in law and government' (in *Life* 275).

Although Smith left Glasgow University in 1764 that was not to be his last contact with the university, because in 1787 he was elected to the honorary post of rector of the university. In a letter of thanks he declares that he remembers his professorial days as 'by far the most useful and therefore as by far the happiest and most honourable period of my life' (*Corr* 309). Smith left Glasgow because he was offered the more lucrative post of tutor and companion to the 18-year-old Duke of Buccleuch. He got this position through the influence of the Duke's step-father, Charles Townsend.

His first task was to take the young duke to France where they settled in Toulouse but little is known of their time there. What is known is that they also resided for a while in Geneva. While there Smith met the most famous French man of letters, François-Marie Arouet (Voltaire) who lived nearby at Ferney and of whom Smith had a high opinion. Armed with introductions, Smith also visited Paris where he mingled with a number of the literary men and some women of the French Enlightenment. Among those he met were the economists Anne-Robert-Jacques Turgot and François Quesnay. He later acknowledged Turgot's assistance in getting information on French taxation (*Corr* 286). Quesnay was the leader of a group of thinkers (the Physiocrats), whose key idea was that agriculture was the stable base of an economy. Smith was familiar with the Physiocrats' arguments. Quesnay, who sent Smith a copy of his *Physiocratie* (1767), was commended in the *Wealth of Nations* as an 'ingenious and profound author' (*WN* 672). Smith, however, was deeply critical of their system and it is an exaggeration to claim that these meetings, and these writings, were decisive in the formation of Smith's own analyses.

Smith's role as tutor was cut short in 1766 by the unfortunate death of his pupil's brother, who had joined them in France. Despite the brevity of his tutorship, Smith was granted a handsome pension (£300) which relieved him of the necessity of having to earn a living. On his return to Scotland he went back to his mother's house in Kirkcaldy, where Smith, speaking retrospectively in 1780, states he used the peace and quiet to write the *Wealth of Nations*. He moved to Edinburgh (taking his mother with him) in 1777 when, again with the support of the Buccleuch connection, he was appointed a customs commissioner. This post paid well and Smith was able to establish himself in a substantial property though not in the fashionable New Town (whither Hume had moved) but in the Canongate area of the Old Town. The job was not a sinecure and Smith was conscientious in his fulfilment of its obligations to such an extent, though with perhaps a hint of disingenuousness, that he judged that it interrupted his 'literary pursuits' (*Corr* 253).

Among these pursuits were preparing further editions of both the *Wealth of Nations* and, especially, the *Moral Sentiments*. He may also at this time have been trying to complete two other manuscripts. The first he identifies as 'a sort of Philosophical History of all the different branches of Literature, of Philosophy, Poetry and Eloquence', the other a 'sort of theory and History of Law and Government' (*Corr* 287). In the end these tasks defeated him. The content of these manuscripts is unknown. Smith instructed his executors to destroy his papers. He did, however, allow that a few could be published and these appeared posthumously as *Essays on Philosophical Subjects* in 1795.

Despite this loss of material, his published work is still extensive and enables a solid assessment to be made of Smith the author. The same cannot be said of Smith the man. He was not a great correspondent and to gauge his personality means relying principally on the testimony of others. Dugald Stewart's *Life* is the most revealing. Stewart observes that Smith's 'private worth' can be vouched for by 'the confidence, respect and attachment which followed him through all the various relations of life'. He had 'many peculiarities' which, reading between the lines, were perhaps off-putting and it was only his 'intimate friends' who were able to appreciate the 'inexpressible charm of his conversation' and 'artless simplicity of his heart' (*Life* 329).

As Stewart continues to depict him, the portrait that emerges is of an introverted, self-contained man, given to absent-mindedness and taciturnity in public. As to his external appearance, all Stewart can say is that 'there was nothing uncommon' about it but does add the profile medallion produced by James Tassie 'conveys an exact idea of his profile' (*Life* 329). Smith never sat for his portrait (itself unusual among his friends) and, aside from Tassie's work, there only exists a stylized memorial print from John Kay (see Figure 1). The statue in Glasgow University is a 19th-century 'imagination' as is the recent (2008) one in Edinburgh.

Scotland in the age of Smith

In what sort of society did Smith live? Although it is a cliché that all ages are times of transition that observation does apply to 18th-century Scotland.

The most momentous political events took place before Smith was born though they were so profound that he lived with the consequences. The genesis lies in the late 17th century. Scotland at that time had its own parliament but a succession of bad harvests, the ruinous collapse of the 'Darien scheme' (the parliament's attempt to establish Scotland as a colonial power), together with a trading dispute with the English supplied a backdrop to the Union of the Parliaments in 1707. Whether the Union was an act of betrayal by some leading Scots, the product of English chicanery, or an 'escape' from immediate pressing difficulties is still a matter of academic (and political) dispute.

The Treaty of Union gave the Scots as Scots little direct political power (only sixteen nobles in the Lords and about 8 per cent of the complement of the Commons). But the Treaty allowed the Scots to retain their own legal system and their own form of church (the kirk) administration and doctrine. These were significant exceptions since it meant that what mattered most immediately to most people remained in Scottish hands. In the absence of a parliament, the lawyers became pivotal figures. On behalf of their patrons, such as notably the Duke of Argyll, they effectively ran Scotland.

When Queen Anne died in 1714 the throne of England and Scotland passed to George of Hanover. This succession had been anticipated in the Treaty because Article II stipulated that should Anne die without issue then the monarchy should pass to Sophia of Hanover and her heirs 'being Protestants'. That article re-affirmed the 1689 Settlement. This document was generated by the accession of William and Mary, following the deposition/abdication of the Stuart king James II/VII, and it stipulated that no Catholic can be monarch. George qualified because being married to a grand-daughter of the first Stuart king (James I and VI) he was the most closely related Protestant. It was the Hanoverian succession that had particular political consequences in Scotland.

The educated, professional Scots, whose many writings across a wide range of subjects constitute the 'Scottish Enlightenment' (as it is now known), were Hanoverians. This meant more than simply supporting the current system because that very support signified their opposition to Jacobitism. The Jacobites were the supporters of the Stuart line and in the first half of the 18th century there were regular flare-ups against the new dynasty. The regularity of these flare-ups suggests that the Hanoverian succession was far from bedded-down.

The two most significant rebellions occurred in 1715 and 1745. The '15 had widespread support, tapping into a well of general dissatisfaction with the perceived lack of benefits flowing from the Union. The '45 initially posed a greater threat to the British state as the army of the Young Pretender or Bonnie Prince Charlie penetrated as far south as Derby in England, about 120 miles from London. The initial military success of the Jacobites was not matched by popular support from the bulk of the Scottish people and was soon reversed. After the battle of Culloden (1746), which crushed the rebellion, it was deliberate government policy to destroy the political separateness of the Highlands.

Smith was in England and away from the turmoil, returning to Kirkcaldy only after Culloden. There is no doubting his loyalty to the Hanoverian regime. In the *Wealth of Nations* he used examples from the Highlands chiefly to illustrate an undeveloped economy and outmoded legal practices. He explicitly mentions Cameron of Lochiel, who without legal authority was able 'to exercise the highest criminal jurisdiction over his own people' (*WN* 416). It wasn't that he was vindictive or capricious but that there was no uniform or functional system of justice owing to the unimproved nature of the infrastructure and economy.

One of the motives behind the Union was the need for Scots to gain unrestricted access to English markets. Conscious of the fact that their economy, when compared to England, was undeveloped, the major Scottish institutions, and their members, sought to modernize or bring about 'improvement'. Eventually, by about mid-century, the Union began to have an economic pay-off and rapid change took place. The growth of Glasgow was the most remarkable of these changes. Its population grew from (roughly) 17,000 when Smith was a student to close to (roughly) 80,000 on his death. Excluding agriculture, the production of textiles, especially linen, was the chief Scottish industry. In Glasgow the crucial development was the growth in the tobacco trade as it overtook Bristol to become the major port. Smith knew a number of the Glasgow 'tobacco lords'. He was a member of the Glasgow Literary Society, presided over by Andrew Cochrane, one of these 'lords'. Their legacy lives on in Glasgow street names, like Glassford and Ingram as well as Cochrane.

The development of 'heavier' industry like coal mining and iron smelting did not take off until the last quarter of the century. The economic principles put forward in the *Wealth of Nations* were not a response to these developments. Smith illustrated his principles with reference to small, workshop manufacture, like pin-making. What urbanization and textile production did require was a supportive infrastructure both physical and financial. Transportation was by horse (Smith rode to Oxford) and boat. While there was a reasonably efficient coach service between Edinburgh and London, cross-country travel was arduous. The simplest way from Kirkcaldy to Edinburgh was by boat across the Firth of Forth rather than by road and ferry.

To transport in bulk had to be by boat and to get from Glasgow to Edinburgh (about 45 miles apart) meant a long and hazardous sea voyage. A crucial 'improving' scheme was to build a canal linking the estuaries of the rivers Forth in the east and the Clyde in the west. This was started in 1768 and completed in 1790. It was a considerable engineering achievement. The still usable viaduct over the river Kelvin near Glasgow was proclaimed as 'one of the most stupendous works of this kind perhaps in the world'. Its construction did, of course, require extensive capital funding. Linked to this need for capital investment was the appearance of many banks. One of the problems faced by the shareholders in the Forth-Clyde Canal was the depression in confidence caused by the crash of the Ayr Bank in 1772. Smith was well aware of these events and his views on speculators ('projectors'), banking, and financial regulation are found in the *Wealth of Nations*.

The officially sanctioned form of church government in Scotland, left intact by the Union, was Presbyterianism of the rigorous Calvinist variety. There was a history of enforced orthodoxy. For example, in 1696 a 19-year-old student Thomas Aikenhead was executed for blasphemy. Yet change was in the air (at least at elite level). The loss of a Scotland's own parliament at the Union enhanced the kirk's role as the nearest equivalent to a national debating forum in the form of the General Assembly. This role made it the focus of political attention and this eventually helped the Scottish church (or elements of it) and the Scottish Enlightenment to come to some sort of mutual understanding. William Robertson personifies this. He was Principal of Edinburgh University for over thirty years and also a leading figure in the reforming or modernizing wing of the church, known as the 'Moderates'. Through astute manoeuvring, this group of like-minded 'modernizers' committed to 'improvement', managed to make itself the dominant 'party' in the Assembly. This enabled the Moderates to oversee the appointment of church ministers sympathetic to improvement and to 'enlightenment'. Smith was friendly with the leading Moderates and this circle was sufficiently catholic (as it were) to include David Hume, popularly regarded as an 'infidel'.

With the exception of Hume and law-lords like Kames, the thinkers of the Scottish Enlightenment were, like Smith, university professors. For a country of Scotland's size and population the presence of five universities—St Andrews, Kings and Marischal Colleges in Aberdeen, and Edinburgh, in addition to Glasgow—is striking. The traditional task of these universities was to turn out

Adam Smith

ministers of religion, and this continued throughout the century but here, too, there was change.

The teaching was reorganized and lectures no longer delivered in Latin (Hutcheson was a pioneer). Professorships in law were established and medical schools were officially recognized in Edinburgh (1740) and Glasgow (1760) (the provision of a medical education, though formally part of the curriculum, had become moribund). This 'vocationalism' was symptomatic of the recognized need to address the demands of social change. Aside from these developments in law and medicine there was expansion in subjects like chemistry and botany which had obvious uses in agricultural improvement, such as the development of fertilizers, and in 'industry', such as dyes for linen. But the universities were also open to intellectual developments. Curricula were changed and especially notable was the speed with which Isaac Newton's work was adopted and professed.

Scotland was a small society and its leading institutions of the law, the church, and the academy formed a network. The intellectual elite were involved across the board. With the involvement of this elite in the key institutions, the Enlightenment in Scotland is an integral part of the 'establishment'. This involvement was given a further expression in the proliferation of clubs and debating societies that formed a point of convergence for the universities, the law, the church and the 'improving' gentry, and, especially in Glasgow, the merchants. For example, the 'Select' Society (or more formally and indicatively 'the Edinburgh Society for the Encouraging of Arts, Sciences, Manufactures and Agriculture') included among its number Smith, Hume, Kames, and Robertson. For all his somewhat retiring nature and reputation, Smith was an active member of several of these associations, not only the Glasgow Literary club with its mix of 'town and gown', but also the convivial as well as intellectual Oyster Club in Edinburgh. He was a founder member of the Royal Society of Edinburgh (1783).

A number of the clubs were concerned with 'politeness'. This reflected the emerging urban culture so that 'urbanity' (and the related 'civility') became positively valued traits of character and behaviour. These are issues that figure prominently in the *Moral Sentiments*.

The Enlightenment: Scotland and beyond

Smith is unquestionably a member of what Peter Gay called the 'Enlightenment family'. The Enlightenment was a self-conscious movement. The participants—referred to in Scotland as the literati—were by definition members of the educated stratum of society. In Scotland they were professionals, especially lawyers, doctors, and university professors, and this is the case elsewhere in Europe, though not in France.

The Enlightenment was not a localized affair. There were family members throughout Europe as well as North America. The literati genuinely were participants in an international dialogue, seeing themselves as engaged in the same debates. One form of this dialogue was direct engagement. So, for example, Smith engaged Jean-Jacques Rousseau by reviewing his *Discourse on Inequality* for the short-lived *Edinburgh Review* in 1755.

A second form of dialogue was the widespread dissemination of works and translations. Both the *Wealth of Nations* and the *Moral Sentiments* were rapidly and widely translated and that added to their dissemination. For example, the Italians typically knew the *Wealth of Nations* via its French version. A good example of this shared intellectual environment is provided by Smith who, on behalf of his university, bought the first seven volumes of Denis Diderot's *Encyclopédie* (begun in 1755). All the Scots expressed their intellectual debt to Charles Secondat, baron Montesquieu, and although Smith (typically) is sparing in his published references to him it is clear from his lecture notes that he had a close knowledge of his work.

Their own imagery of 'light' provides a helpful clue to the core concerns of these self-conscious intellectuals. Light implied that earlier times were comparatively benighted. In less metaphorical terms this contrast between light and dark is the contrast between knowledge or reason on the one hand and ignorance, prejudice, and superstition on the other. Slavery, torture, witchcraft, religious persecution, and the like were to be opposed as relics, as creatures of the night.

Smith's writings show that he shared this agenda. Even though as a writer he was not given to expressions of outrage he was clear that slavery is evil, was unambiguous in his condemnation of infanticide, and fervent in his denunciation of judicial cruelty. In this last case he drew on personal experience. While in Toulouse, Jean Calas, a Calvinist, was falsely accused and then executed by the local Catholic authorities for the supposed murder of his son (Smith added a reference to this event in the final edition of the *Moral Sentiments*).

Central to the lifting of darkness was the light shone by science. The brightest star in that firmament was Isaac Newton. Newton was the hero of the Enlightenment. His achievement was to encompass within one comprehensive schema an explanation, derived from a few simple principles (laws of motion plus gravity), of the range of natural phenomena, from the orbit of the planets to apples falling from trees. Crucially and decisively these laws were proved to be right. Newton's calculation that the Earth was, contrary to the system of the French mathematician and philosopher René Descartes, more like a turnip (flatter around the poles) than a lemon (elongated at the poles) was vindicated by scientific expeditions to Lapland and the Equator. One hallmark of Newton's status was that to liken someone's work to his was to pay it the highest possible compliment. For example, John Millar in his *Historical View* (1787) declared Smith to be the 'Newton of political economy' because he had discovered the principles of commerce. Smith shared this Enlightenment enthusiasm and in his case this was backed up by an impressive knowledge of astronomy.

The Scots believed in progress. This belief required an account of social change over time and much of the writing of the Scottish Enlightenment pursued this project. It was a conspicuous feature of Smith's university lectures and is an important theme in the *Wealth of Nations*. The Scots had a relatively cautious conception of progress. They accept that much light has been shed across a wide front and that the growth of knowledge is indeed a crucial ingredient in this advance. However, they are less confident than some of their contemporaries in France or England that progress is automatic and necessarily always and in all respects an improvement. An important factor accounting for their caution is that the Scots attach weight to the role of social habits or customs, which are resistant to obvious or quick solutions. In line with this Smith emphasizes the gradualness of social change and argues that the change itself is often an unintended consequence. These emphases run though all of his work.

Chapter 2
Communication and imagination

In the breadth of his interests and knowledge, Adam Smith was a typical member of the Enlightenment. Today he is best known as an economist but that is to short-change him. Something important is missed if the rest of his work is not taken on board. Not only does this neglect the range of his thinking it also obscures its interwoven character. The arguments in the *Moral Sentiments* and the *Wealth of Nations* intersect and his posthumously published *Essays on Philosophical Subjects* throw light on recurrent themes in his work.

One of these themes is that humans are social beings. Smith investigates forms of social interaction, like buying and selling or praising and blaming, but he also looks, more generally, at how humans try to make sense of the world around them and of one another in it. Precisely because they are social creatures, humans do not, and cannot, do this on their own. They have to interact or communicate. This general question features prominently in the *Essays* as well as in some of his Glasgow lectures.

Language

An obviously central aspect of communication is language. Prior to his appointment at Glasgow, Smith gave some public lectures on rhetoric in Edinburgh. In the more formal setting of the university lecture hall, he returned to the subject. Thanks to the discovery of student notes, there is a record of his lectures in 1762–3. One of these lectures was devoted to the origin of language. Of the thirty lectures that have survived this was the only one that he thought worthwhile expanding and publishing. The 'Considerations concerning the First Formation of Languages and the different genius of Original and Compounded Languages' first appeared in a book of philological essays published in London in 1761 and then as an appendix to the third edition (1767) of the *Moral Sentiments*.

Why publish this particular lecture? Two general reasons suggest themselves. The great fear of the Scottish literati was that they would appear provincial and unpolished when compared to the more fashionable centres of London and Paris. This anxiety fuelled a preoccupation with how to write in correct English in order to avoid what were called 'Scotticisms'. David Hume, for example, compiled a list of these as did his arch-philosophical foe James Beattie. They also wished to avoid sounding uncouth when they spoke. Classes on elocution were given in Edinburgh and drew large audiences.

Smith was not immune to this general anxiety but the second reason is more important. The whole question of the origin of language was a subject of lively debate across the Enlightenment, and by choosing to publish the *Considerations* Smith was declaring himself a participant. The *Considerations* do not make a significant contribution to the history of linguistics, though the same can be said of most the debate's participants. However, the work is informative because it outlines a pattern of thinking that recurs across his writings.

In the *Considerations* Smith approaches his subject from two complementary directions. His treatment is both philosophical or theoretical and historical or empirical. The common thread is the development of grammar. The theoretical argument is that the

16

various grammatical elements in language (verbs, nouns, adjectives, prepositions, etc.) are not all present at the beginning of human speech. Rather, they develop or emerge alongside the maturing of human faculties. The essay plots this development.

Smith's template (so to speak) for this was an adaptation of the argument of the English philosopher John Locke (1632–1704). Locke was an empiricist (holding that what we know is the product of our experience). He illustrated this with a well-known image. Humans are born as a blank sheet of paper on which is written what is acquired initially through our senses (sight, touch, etc.).

Following Locke, Smith (along with many others) drew a parallel between the development of language in children and its development in humankind. This parallel relies on 'savages' representing, in a favourite phrase in the Enlightenment (and in Scotland especially), 'the infancy of mankind'. *Both* children and savages live in the 'here and now', a world of immediate sensations. They dwell in the present and because of their undeveloped faculties they neither ruminate on the past nor plan for the future. Any such rumination or planning supposes on their part a capacity for reflection, an ability to distance or abstract themselves from what currently grabs their attention. But just as children grow up and enlarge their experience, so, too, language develops.

According to Smith this process occurs 'insensibly' by which he means that it is not a product of self-conscious reasoning. It just happens in the natural course of things. His developmental argument rules out reasoning because it would mean, contrary to the evidence, that children and savages are capable of thinking abstractly or, in their initial utterances, of using general terms.

Smith applies this argument to the various parts of speech. His model is Latin and that language supplies most of his examples.

Nouns begin as words that refer to a particular object in a particular location at a particular time. This is the initial language of children and savages. But as experience grows, that same word would be generalized 'naturally' (or insensibly) and be given to similar features regardless of time or place.

He gives the word 'tree' as an example. At first it referred only to a particular object but over time the word is applied to similar objects and gradually becomes a general or abstract term referring to any or all trees. The abstract noun 'tree' similarly predates the more abstract adjective 'green' which itself precedes the even more abstract word 'greenness'. Smith makes clear the assumptions underlying this developmental process when he treats prepositions and pronouns. These parts of speech, he declares, because they are 'the most general and abstract...would probably be the last invented'; they would 'not easily or readily occur to the first formers of language' (CL 212, 219). What would more readily occur is changing the endings of an existing word. The separate word 'of', for example, is a later development than the creation of a genitive case.

This same developmental process also applies to verbs. At first savages would convey the approach of a lion (Smith's example) in a single word. In due course that word would be generalized to refer to the approach of any wild beast (itself a concurrent generalization) and gradually be generalized further to refer simply or purely to the act of approaching. As experience enlarges, instead of a single word there develop nouns (lion) and pronouns (I/you approach), as well as auxiliaries (he had approached).

It is typical of Smith's thought that this account of the evolution of grammar is complemented by historical evidence. Travellers and historians all report that in the languages of savages there is, for example, an absence of personal pronouns and when they developed any new words they did this by amending existing ones. Ancient Greek is a case a point, it is a simple or uncompounded language (this explains the reference to 'compounded' languages in the full title of the *Considerations*). But as society develops and tribes interact, languages mix. This leads to a simplification of grammar.

This time using Greek as his example, Smith observes that this language has a complex system of conjugations and declensions. In contrast, English, as a mix of French and Saxon, possesses a large vocabulary and, as a result, is grammatically a much simpler language. This greater simplicity followed from the need to interact. In order for the speakers of two different languages to communicate they had to forgo mastering the intricacies of the other language. It is in this way, Smith conjectures, that a preposition ('of') would 'naturally' replace the genitive case in a declension. This empirical/historical account thus comes to the same conclusion as his philosophical analysis of grammar.

Since humans are social beings then this use of increasingly abstract terms and simplified grammar occurs and evolves in that setting. Smith's argument in the *Considerations* is an example of 'conjectural' (or theoretical or natural) history, as Dugald Stewart called it when making explicit reference to this work. This style of argument and its developmental assumptions recur throughout Smith's work. For example, in the *Wealth of Nations* Smith traces the development of money as a unit of exchange from concrete material objects, like shells, to inherently worthless pieces of paper or to the even more abstract idea of credit. Again, political rule develops from the tangible personal physical power exercised by the strong to the abstract impersonal authority of the rule of law.

A central theme of conjectural history is that humans start off thinking in practical terms about their immediate circumstances (what's the best way to catch fish?). But as society develops they can stand back from the demands of daily life and think more theoretically as they begin to reflect on their circumstances (why can't fish live out of water?).

Association and explanation

The link between increased reflectiveness and social development is a feature of the 'History of Astronomy' (one of his posthumously published *Essays*). In the third section of the 'Astronomy' Smith again refers to the life of the 'savage'. Savages, he conjectures, live in a pre-philosophical age where subsistence is precarious and life is short. They are preoccupied with immediate questions of survival and have neither the time nor the inclination to look into the causes of things. When confronted by startling irregularities in their experience, their response is to invoke some 'invisible and designing power' (HA 49). This invocation is based on their own emotions such as fear or love. If the sea is stormy then Neptune is angry, if calm then it expresses his good will. In this anthropomorphism Smith sees the origin of polytheism, separate gods responsible for harvests or the quality of the wine or the variability of the weather and so on. He makes much the same point in the *Moral Sentiments*.

However, with the gradual establishment of order and security there comes, for those of 'liberal fortunes', sufficient leisure to enable them to pay closer and more reflective attention to the world around them. This 'attention', Smith declares, is a disinterested affair. As befits the social status of its first practitioners, philosophy or science (the terms are interchangeable) does not originate in any material need to extract advantage from its discoveries. To investigate why fish have gills is a distinct enquiry from how to increase the catch. That humans can have motives beyond meeting their immediate needs is an argument Smith will make in the *Wealth of Nations*.

The first societies developed enough to practise philosophy were the city-states of Greece and their colonies. The final section of the essay is devoted to the history of astronomy as a test-case of this philosophical development. Smith charts its history from the system of concentric circles of Aristotle through Ptolemy to Copernicus, Galileo, Kepler, Descartes, and finally Newton. Although his scholarship is remarkable what is of most interest is Smith's discussion in the opening sections of the essay. In these sections Smith puts forward a general psychological argument.

He is attempting to account for a distinctive feature of human nature: why are humans always looking for explanations? It is this attempt that is captured in the full title of the essay 'The Principles which lead and direct Philosophical Enquiries: Illustrated by the History of Astronomy'. There are two other shorter essays included in the posthumous collection that also 'illustrate' these 'principles', namely, 'Ancient Physics' and 'Ancient Logics and Metaphysics', but they scarcely live up to their billing being far sketchier and limited in subject-matter. All three are investigations into motivation, into what 'leads' humans to philosophize. Smith is explicit about that remit. He is not assessing astronomical systems and is explicit that it is a separate question as to whether or not these systems are true or consistent with reality.

As in the *Considerations*, in the 'Astronomy' there is an underlying acceptance of an empirical, Lockean approach. Indeed the parallel between the savage and the child is repeated when he notes how a child 'beats the stone that hurts it' and the savage punishes the axe that had accidentally caused a death (HA 49). The underlying assumption, which Smith took from David Hume's amendment of the Lockean approach, is that in the normal run of things humans out of habit expect events to follow a sequence. To give one of Hume's examples, first flame then heat; we link or associate them in that order because it is a constant feature of experience that the latter follows the former.

As Smith himself explains,

> when two objects, however unlike, have often been observed to
> follow each other, and have constantly presented themselves to the
> senses in that order they come to be so connected together in the
> fancy [imagination] that the idea of the one seems of its own accord
> to call up and introduce that of the other.   (HA 40)

The effect of this 'habit of the imagination' is a putting together of
recurrent features of experience, it categorizes or classifies them.
Smith illustrates this with an example drawn from language.
Echoing the example of 'tree' in the *Considerations*, he here cites
the word 'animal' as a general name that classifies or groups
together by association all those beings that move of their own
accord. It is what happens when these habitual acts of association
break down that interests Smith. For example, in the 18th century
whether a polyp was an animal or a vegetable was hotly debated
(Smith alludes to this).

He starts by identifying three human sentiments—surprise,
wonder, and admiration. He then elaborates. Surprise is
experienced when the unexpected happens, wonder is excited
by what is new and singular, and admiration by what is
great and beautiful. The first two emotions do most of the
work in Smith's argument as it unfolds. Having provided this
psychological sentimental foundation he can proceed with
his inquiry.

In line with his definitions, when the habitual or expected
associations break down, or when an event or object eludes the
customary categories or groupings, we are 'at first surprised by
the unexpectedness of the new appearances' (HA 41). The next
step is crucial. Once the momentary emotion of surprise passes
then, he asserts, we wonder how the unexpected event came
about. Wonder is stimulated when an aspect of experience
appears incoherent, or in other words when there are gaps or

breaks that disrupt the associations made by the smooth working of the imagination.

For Smith this disruption and inability to classify creates 'uncertainty and anxious curiosity' (HA 40). Why? His answer relies on the incontrovertible fact that humans seek pleasure and avoid pain. This reliance is a constant in his work, underpinning, for example, much of the argument in *The Theory of Moral Sentiments*. Anxiety or unease is a species of pain from which it follows that there is a motive to remove or alleviate it. A remedy is sought. The remedy on offer is to provide an explanation. The source of the human motivation to explain is an emotional impulse to plug these gaps and in that way dispel anxiety and restore the pleasurable default state of orderly associations. How is this restoration achieved?

Smith's answer is striking. He says the gap is plugged by supposing or imagining a connection. The associations that the imagination has customarily made are replicated by supposing a 'chain of intermediate, though invisible, events' (HA 42). He gives the example of magnetism. To see iron seemingly of itself move toward a lodestone breaks the established (by habit) associations that account for the motion of an object as a result of it being either pulled or pushed. That break or gap creates an uneasiness that needs to be removed. In this case the associational gap is bridged by imagining some invisible medium that connects (pulls) the iron to the lodestone. The effect of this act of imagination is that this connection can now be classified as a familiar example of motion as the effect of some impulse. This imagined chain creates a new set of customary associations and the painful incoherence of gaps removed. Once this is achieved then the movement of the iron has been explained. It is no longer surprising and a cause of wonder.

Smith took this example from René Descartes (1596–1650). Descartes' solution to the 'problem of magnetism' was clearly a more sophisticated gap-filling than the savage's invocation of some god. This relative sophistication reflects social development. As society develops so a distinction implicitly emerges between experts and others. Non-experts, that is 'the bulk of mankind', typically experience no breaks in their imagined associations. Smith remarks that humans in general do not 'wonder' how what they eat is converted into muscle or fat. By contrast experts are 'embarrassed' by incoherencies and seek to unite 'the various appearances of nature'.

Philosophers or scientists are experts who seek to unify this variety. Smith defines philosophy as the 'science of the connecting principles of nature' (HA 45). Like Descartes' explanation of magnetic attraction, it introduces order into chaos by 'representing the invisible chains' that bind together disjointed objects. In this way philosophy/science allays the 'tumult of the imagination' and restores it to tranquillity. On this basis, Smith now affirms, philosophy can be 'regarded as one of those arts which address themselves to the imagination' (HA 46). The history of astronomy is an 'illustration' of this process. In telling this story Smith draws particular attention to the transition from one astronomical system to another.

The Copernican heliocentric system replaced Ptolemy's geocentric model. But that success did not happen overnight. Smith astutely observes that it was initially rejected not only by the ignorant but also by the 'learned' whose own habits of imagination resisted Copernicus' re-imagining. But there were exceptions among the learned and in time, as more evidence accumulated, more and more astronomers accepted Copernicus. This was not the end of the matter. The Copernican system continued to create for astronomers (experts) more wonder, more gaps in an imagined chain. In accordance with Smith's psychological theory these, too, had to be bridged. For example, the gap between the revolutionary motion of the planets and their supposed inertness made the scientists uneasy. Their imagination was disturbed. Descartes attempted to restore tranquillity by conceiving the planets as floating in a substance he called 'ether'. This had some success because it was an analogy (a form of classification) familiar to the imagination (heavy objects like ships can float). Yet Smith remarks that this success was short-lived. Descartes proposed gap-filling was almost universally rejected in favour of Newton's.

The advantages of the Newtonian system are that it explained all planetary irregularities (something Descartes failed to do). Its predictions had proved accurate and it had linked into one system all celestial and terrestrial phenomena. Newton had achieved this by utilizing the principle of gravity. Because this is so familiar, after all apples when detached from their branch always fall to the ground they do not fly into the sky, then it was easy to imagine it as an explanatory principle. In consequence, Smith declares, here echoing the standard Enlightenment judgment, that Newton's work was 'the greatest and most admirable improvement that was ever made in philosophy' (HA 98). This is true not only as a matter of demonstrable fact but also in terms of the essay's remit to investigate the psychological underpinnings of the motivation to philosophize. Newton has restored tranquillity.

In general, if not in specific, terms Smith aimed to follow a Newtonian methodology. According to Newton himself in his *Principia* (1686), the first rule of reasoning in natural philosophy is: admit only such causes as are 'true and sufficient to explain appearances'. Here two points are being made—the aim should be economy so that a lot is explained by a little and the explanation is achieved through the identification of causes.

Smith says of the 'Astronomy' that his aim in that essay is to consider the 'nature and causes' of the three emotions and their influence. That same terminology is reflected in the full title of his most famous work as *An Inquiry into the Nature and Causes of the Wealth of Nations*. This repetition is no coincidence; it reflects the interwoven character of Smith's work. One clear illustration of this is his comment in the *Wealth of Nations* that the 'revolutions of the heavenly bodies ... necessarily excite wonder so they naturally call forth the curiosity of mankind to enquire into their causes' (*WN* 767).

Style and aesthetics

More evidence of Smith's endorsement of Newton can be found in his Logic class at Glasgow. According to John Millar (as reported to Dugald Stewart), Smith in that class concentrated on rhetoric and belles-lettres. In this course of lectures, Smith explicitly identified a particular style of writing as the 'Newtonian method'. This method he judged to be the 'most philosophical'. It proceeds from proven first principles to explain a variety of phenomena by 'connecting [them] altogether by the same chain' (*LRBL* 146). This last phrase reveals a link to the *Astronomy*. For example, in the context of historical composition, he remarks that 'the very notion of a gap makes us uneasy' (*LRBL* 100).

Though Smith is not explicit, the inference is that Newton's method should be followed in 'every science' whether 'natural' (like physics) or 'social' (like economics). This inference is strengthened when the Newtonian method is compared to its chief alternative, the Aristotelian. The latter method, Smith identifies as one where a different principle is given to every phenomenon. It is deficient both because it is unsystematic and because it lacks the economy of the Newtonian approach.

Millar also reports that, given the youthfulness of his student audience, it was Smith's view that his emphasis on rhetoric was,

> the best method of explaining and illustrating [that] the various powers of the human mind ... arises from an examination of the several ways of communicating our thoughts by speech, and from an attention to the principles of those literary compositions which contribute to persuasion or entertainment. (*Life* 274)

Language as a basic form of human communication involves more than the grammatical analysis undertaken in the *Considerations*. As social beings, humans use it to persuade, cajole, inspire, and so on; they practise rhetoric. The art of rhetoric had a long history. To speak persuasively was the key to political and legal success in Greece and Rome and numerous 'how to' books were written. The study of rhetoric was institutionalized in the Renaissance and it continued as a staple of education. But Smith, along with many of his contemporaries and compatriots, changed the focus. The emphasis in the majority of his lectures was on literature (belles-lettres), on written rather than verbal communication.

Literary style thus becomes a key topic. For Smith, stylistic 'perfection' consists in authors expressing concisely their meaning and doing so in a way that best conveys the 'sentiment, passion or affection' they want to communicate to the reader (*LRBL* 55). The communication of sentiments plays a key role in the *Moral Sentiments*. In the rhetoric lectures the focus is on the link between style and aesthetic taste because a successful communication would have 'all the beauty language was capable of bestowing on it' (*LRBL* 40). In the terminology of the 'Astronomy', it calls forth admiration. The analysis of style becomes in this way a major feature of literary criticism. For example, Smith criticized Lord Shaftesbury's 'pompous, grand and ornate' style as inappropriate when writing philosophically where precision is required (*LRBL* 59). It is, however, not obvious that Smith himself in his published works, especially in the *Moral Sentiments*, obeyed this own injunction to avoid embellishment.

Another essay in the posthumous collection pursued some of these questions in a more abstract manner. One of these, 'Of the Imitative Arts', deals with a central question in contemporary aesthetics. Smith distinguishes between 'servile imitation', where an exact resemblance or perfect copy is the aim, and a superior type of imitation which seeks to resemble 'an object of a different

27

kind', whether 'a production of nature or art' (IA 178). The superiority is clearest when there is a disparity between the imitated and the imitation.

He gives one of Rembrandt's paintings as a particular example of this disjunction. Rembrandt, as a sophisticated artist, has exhibited great skill in depicting 'a vulgar ordinary man or woman, engaged in a vulgar ordinary action' (IA 179). This juxtaposition for Smith lies at the root of aesthetic pleasure. The same viewer who delights in the picture would (by implication) look upon its subject matter, these ordinary folk in the flesh, with distaste. In now familiar language, Smith says we 'wonder' at the effect created and are pleased when we appreciate, to some extent at least, how it was achieved. In this way the 'pleasing wonder of ignorance is accompanied with the still more pleasing satisfaction of science' (IA 185). The essay proceeds to outline how imitation differs between the arts with an annexed section that deals specifically with music, dancing, and poetry.

This essay, alongside his belle-lettristic concern with literature, supports Dugald Stewart's observation that Smith 'never neglected to cultivate a taste for the fine arts' (*Life* 305). These particular concerns testify to the breadth of Smith's own interests. They also reveal, more generally, the importance he gives to communication. Reflecting the interwoven character of his work, this commitment to the importance of communication pervades more than his writing and teaching on language and rhetoric. It also informs his two best-known works; for example, in his account of the dynamics of exchange (a form of persuasion) in the *Wealth of Nations* and, along with imagination, in the dynamics of moral assessment in the *Moral Sentiments*.

Chapter 3
Sympathetic spectators

Smith published *The Theory of Moral Sentiments* in 1759. It drew heavily on his university lectures, following his appointment as Professor of Moral Philosophy in 1752. The book went through six editions in his lifetime, with the second (1761) and sixth (published in 1790, the year of his death) making significant changes. The third (1767) included the 'Considerations on Language', although modern editions omit it and re-locate it in the *Lectures on Rhetoric and Belles-Lettres*. Since Smith continued to work on his moral philosophy after the publication of the *Wealth of Nations* in 1776, then it is reasonable enough to assume there is no fundamental rift between his 'economics' and 'ethics'.

Empiricism

The title *The Theory of Moral Sentiments* is revealing. Smith's decision to call it a 'theory' tells the reader that it is work of enquiry or philosophy. At the same time it implies that it is not a guidebook instructing the reader how to live morally. Perhaps, because many other 18th-century works on 'morality' were 'how to' manuals of that sort, Smith added a sub-title to the third edition. This announced that the book was 'An Essay towards an Analysis of the Principles by which Men naturally judge concerning the Conduct and Character, first of their Neighbours, and afterwards of themselves'. What the book sets out to do is investigate or analyse how, in practice, judgments and decisions about what is right or wrong are made.

The term 'sentiments' in the book's title is also informative. It locates the book in a particular tradition of moral philosophy and one that was especially strong in Scotland. The Scots are empiricists, that is knowledge derives from experience (cf. Chapter 2). We know rain is wet because we feel it on our skin; we know that the ancient Romans wore togas because we have evidence from statuary and literature; we know that the tribes of North America are war-like because we have corroboratory evidence from missionaries and explorers. Moral knowledge is no exception. According to the Scots' moral philosophy, the evidence is that humans experience and respond to the world through feeling or emotion or sentiment. We all feel anger towards cheats, we all feel affection to those who support us, we all feel compassion toward the unfortunate, and so on.

Feelings or emotions act as motives. We are moved to anger. What moves humans are their desires or passions. Here the Scottish empiricists hit a problem. The source of this problem was the reading of the 'evidence' that was put forward by two (non-Scottish) thinkers in particular—Thomas Hobbes (1588–1679) and Bernard Mandeville (1670–1733). The agenda for the Scots' moral philosophy, including Smith's, was developed in response to their argument.

For Hobbes *the* fact about humans is that they are concerned with their own well-being or self-interest to the exclusion of others. Each and every person is motivated by their passions: if they want something they are driven toward obtaining it; and, conversely, if they are afraid they are driven away from what scares them. As an account of motivation, with one crucial exception, there was nothing here to which Smith and others would object. The exception was Hobbes' insistence on exclusivity. According to Hobbes individuals were always either actually or potentially in competition with each other. His solution to that unbridled competition was to establish an authorized sovereign, who would enforce 'fair play' or, more broadly, end disputes about justice or what is right and good.

For contemporaries and successors this was unacceptable because it reduced morality to doing what the sovereign said. One influential counter to Hobbes was given by Anthony Ashley Cooper, third Earl of Shaftesbury (1671–1713). Shaftesbury thought Hobbes' philosophy rested on a faulty reading of human nature. Humans were not exclusively self-centred; they also possessed what he called a 'natural moral sense'. Here Shaftesbury introduced the terminology that the Scots would adopt.

The Scots openly acknowledge their debt to Shaftesbury but this is mediated by the impact of Mandeville. Like Hobbes but in an even more openly provocative manner, Mandeville argued that virtuous actions were not necessary to produce beneficial outcomes, vices can have the same effect. For example, greed is good because it generates material prosperity. To his contemporaries this was tantamount to saying virtue was a sham and that the virtuous (all right-thinking individuals in other words) were hypocrites. Certainly Mandeville made Shaftesbury a frequent target for such jibes. But what was so potentially damaging was Mandeville's claim that Shaftesbury's theory is untrue because it is inconsistent with daily experience.

Pre-eminent among the defenders of Shaftesbury against Mandeville was Francis Hutcheson, Smith's teacher and predecessor as Professor of Moral Philosophy. While there is more to Hutcheson than a negative reaction to Mandeville, this context is central to his own positive moral theory and that theory is in its turn central to all the Scots. This does not mean they agree with him but their own thoughts are shaped by the ways in which they disagree. Smith's moral philosophy follows that pattern.

Hutcheson and moral sense

In contrast to Hobbes and Mandeville, Hutcheson firmly separates morality from 'advantage' or self-interest. He announces that his intention is to seek to discover the natural foundation for moral goodness (and moral evil). He finds this foundation in the moral sense possessed by all humans. In the way that the five senses of smell, sight, etc. tell humans about the physical world around them, so Hutcheson argues the moral sense tells them about human conduct. Moreover, just as we cannot help seeing what we see when our eyes are open, we cannot help determining whether an action is good or not. Importantly this 'determination' (Hutcheson's word) is made without any reference to personal advantage. An adaptation of one of his examples captures what is at stake. Suppose Aaron and Zoe each give me £100. Aaron does so because he wishes me to be happy, Zoe because she calculates giving the £100 will further her self-interest. Although I get £100 in each case, according to Hutcheson I will have a different sentiment toward Aaron than I do toward Zoe. That 'difference', he declares, is perceived by the moral sense.

The whole thrust of Hutcheson's argument is that the principle of self-interest is unable to explain moral experience. We feel there is a real difference between the benevolent action of Aaron and the self-serving behaviour of Zoe. For Hutcheson benevolence lies at the core of morality, this is what the moral sense identifies. Benevolence, literally good will toward 'all beings capable of happiness or misery', is not something humans have to learn. It is instinctive. But here Smith disagrees, as does David Hume, the most important link between Smith and Hutcheson.

Sympathy

Although Hutcheson had used the term 'sympathy' it played a central role in Hume's empiricist moral philosophy. For him it is the means by which we pass moral judgments. Sympathy converts knowledge of a crime into the sentiment that a wrong has been done. By calling this a conversion he is departing from Hutcheson's direct recourse to the moral sense. Sympathy is the key idea in Smith's own philosophy but he differs from Hutcheson and Hume's accounts.

When Smith first refers to sympathy he defines it as 'our fellow-feeling with any passion whatever' (*TMS* 10). This, however, is misleadingly simple. For both Hutcheson and Hume sympathy was likened to a sort of contagion or infection. Smith's opening discussion seems similar. He talks of a transfusion of emotions when observers themselves sway in step with the movements of a tight-rope walker. But Smith's analysis is not based on an infectious or direct transfusion of sentiments. He interposes a decisive intermediary. In Smith's account of sympathy imagination plays this mediating role.

All human beings can imagine how they would feel if they were in the situation of another. They proceed on the working assumption that everyone pretty much feels the same way about the same sort of things. To give one of Smith's own examples: if I see someone in distress because they have learnt of the death of their father I can imagine how I would feel if I was the situation of the bereaved. It is the situation or context that is crucial. Smith stresses that 'sympathy' in his technical sense is not based solely on another's exhibited passion (sobbing in grief). If that was the case then it would be a kind of contagion or transfusion. Instead, it is through the intervention of our imagination that we bring 'home to our own breast' the other's sensations or passions (*TMS* 17–18).

This 'bringing home' is no direct replication. There are two reasons why. The emotion that is brought home is generated not only by the exhibited passion (visible distress) but by the total 'situation'. Is it in a public or private space? How recent is knowledge of the death? Also our emotion necessarily takes on a weaker form, it is not my father who has died. Both the contextual setting and the relative lack of intensity come to play an important role in sympathetic interactions.

Smith's next move is critical and what turns his analysis from psychology to moral philosophy. He talks of the interaction between actors and spectators. It is the latter who use their imagination to bring home the contextually or situationally expressed emotions of the former. Once brought home spectators are in a position to assess the actor's emotions. By imagining themselves to be the actors they can judge whether in context the actor has behaved appropriately or, in Smith's terms, with propriety. If so then they approve. To return to Smith example: I approve of the grief exhibited by the newly bereaved within the context of their family and friends. Conversely, without any more knowledge, I would disapprove if someone in that situation showed signs of joy.

This is why the medical metaphor of transfusion or contagion is misleading. Smith notes that spectators can blush for the impudence of the actors even though they are not aware of the crassness of their behaviour. What makes this possible is that humans learn from experience. They learn which situations typically generate what sort of emotions and how those emotions are typically expressed. Hence sadness follows parental death and that is felt more intensely than (say) disappointment that one's orchid has failed to flower. Where is this learnt? For an empiricist like Smith, the only source is from the experience of everyday life in society. This sociality is decisive.

Sociality

Smith likens society to a mirror. He supposes that if someone grew up in isolation then just as they would have no idea of whether they were beautiful or ugly nor would they have any idea as to whether or not they were acting morally. But

> [b]ring him into society and he is immediately provided with the mirror which he wanted before... and all his own passions will immediately become the causes of new passions. He will observe that mankind approve of some of them and are disgusted by others. He will be elevated in the one case, and cast down in the other; his desires and aversions, his joys and sorrows, will now often become the causes of new desires and new aversions, new joys and new sorrows: they will now, therefore, interest him deeply, and often call upon his most attentive consideration. (*TMS* 110)

This is an important passage.

It reveals Smith's account of motivation and his basic empiricist credentials. This can be seen in his use of the words 'passions', 'desires', and 'aversions'. He says unequivocally later in the book that 'pleasure and pain are the great objects of desire and aversion' (*TMS* 320). It is an indisputable fact of human behaviour that humans enjoy pleasure and thus desire it, while conversely they dislike pain and thus strive to avoid it. These emotions are what 'move' us, they are the causes of our actions. Since, according to this passage, we feel 'elevated' when our actions are approved (my poem is praised) it follows that approval is pleasing (I am happy when my poetry is well received). And because pleasure is a motive then, it further follows, that humans desire approval (I want to write poetry that is praised and not dismissed as doggerel).

The importance of this passage also stems from its description of an interactive learning process. To live in society is to take part in a network of communication, to receive and send information about how to behave in different situations. From the messages received from others, I learn that some of my actions are approved, and some disapproved. Since I want to do what pleases and avoid what causes me pain, I am motivated to repeat the former and avoid the latter. In this way I react to the communicative signal sent. I acquire knowledge of what behaviour is condoned or condemned in given situations. This acquisition, in other words, gives us our moral compass.

Morality is inseparable from sociality. This marks one of Smith's clear departures from Hutcheson's moral sense, which operates 'antecedent to instruction'. This was also Hume's view but Smith's account was more thoroughly worked out. For Smith there is no need to invoke a special sense to identify good and evil, since the communicative give-and-take of sentiments engaged in by spectators and actors is sufficient to produce moral judgment.

This communicative interaction is educative; it is the way we all learn how to act as members of a society. But social learning is not like school-learning. It is indirect and is absorbed through exposure to everyday life rather than through a text-book or class-room instruction. In the 18th century the effect produced by this exposure was referred to as 'moral causation'. The use of 'moral' here refers to its etymological origin in the Latin for custom (*mos/morem*). To refer to this as 'causation' signals that character, opinions, and values are formed to a large extent by the social environment. It is not, however, a rigid form of determinism (what was called 'physical causation') as when heat causes the body to sweat.

Smith gives a particularly striking example of moral causation at work in the *Wealth of Nations* but one that he had already used in his Glasgow jurisprudence lectures, which he delivered alongside his moral philosophy class. He compares the 'most dissimilar characters' of a philosopher and a 'common street porter'. This dissimilarity he says derives 'not so much from nature as from habit, custom and education'. Indeed in his university lectures he puts this more emphatically; what in their maturity, 'appears to distinguish men of different professions' is upon many occasions 'not so much the cause as the effect of the division of labour' (*WN* 28–9; *LJ* 348). In Smith's example it is as soon as infants enter employment that they begin to differ as the habits and demands of different occupations take hold. One is not 'born' but 'made' a philosopher (or porter).

Negotiated concord

For Smith, experience tells us that a spectator's emotions are less intense than those of the actor. This fact about human nature is accompanied with another. The actor wishes (because it pleases) the spectator's sympathetic approval. There is, though, from the actor's perspective a gap or shortfall between these two facts. Since the first, different degrees of intensity, is unalterable then it is the second, seeking approval, where the actor's efforts must lie. Smith employs musical metaphors to convey his point.

In order to bring about 'harmony and concord' between their emotions and those of the spectator, and thus achieve the desired approval, actors must lower their passion to that 'pitch' that enables spectators to go along with them (*TMS* 22). To revert again to the earlier example: if the grief at parental death is too demonstrative, full of public cries of anguish and lamentation, then the spectator may judge this excessive and withhold the desired approval. To arrive at the appropriate 'pitch' is to achieve not perfect accord or unison but concord or sufficient agreement to enable peaceable coexistence. This achievement is not automatic but a negotiation; once again, it is the fruit of social learning.

This negotiated pitch is not fixed but will differ between situations. For example, the socially approved public response to grief will differ between Scotland and Syria. There is one difference that is especially important. The extent of the negotiation will depend on the relationship between the actor and spectator. We can express our feelings more openly and fully in the presence of those to whom we are emotionally close. When grieving the death of a parent before other members of the family the pitch can be much higher—the negotiated concord will take less effort.

Smith puts a historical gloss on this. He supposes that in earlier simpler ages, where dealings with family and friends dominate, plenty of sympathy will be forthcoming. Concord will be relatively easy to achieve. The counterpart to this is that more effort is needed to 'tone down' the emotions when in 'an assembly of strangers' (*TMS* 23). Concord in that situation is harder to attain. This is the prevailing situation in a complicated, modern society, what Smith calls a commercial society. The *Wealth of Nations* analyses that type of society but it is also the backdrop to the *Moral Sentiments*. Within commercial societies self-interest looms large.

Self-interest

Smith is clear that Hobbes and Mandeville are wrong. Humans are not exclusively motivated by self-interest. He devoted a whole section of the *Moral Sentiments* to a criticism of what he calls Mandeville's 'licentious system'. Smith's fundamental opposition is announced in the opening sentence of the book,

> How selfish soever a man may be supposed, there are evidently some principles in his nature which interest him in the fortune of others, and render their happiness necessary to him, though he derive nothing from it except the pleasure of seeing it,   (*TMS* 9)

Smith is here clearly following Hutcheson's lead. Everything we know about human experience confirms that everyone, just like Aaron, can express a genuine disinterested concern for the happiness of others.

This opening sentence does, however, leave room for other 'principles'. Among these Smith, and other empiricists, include self-love. But this inclusion seemed to create a problem or a weakness. Smith, Hutcheson, and Hume all think that consulting reason cannot tell humans what they should do. For those thinkers who do think reason has that power morality is a matter of objective truth. The relation between murder and wrong is like the ratio of a diameter to a circumference, its truth does not depend on any facts of experience. The Scots reject this argument. Their empiricism means experience is what counts. And because experience is gained via the senses or feelings then they had to locate morality in the subjective realm of sentiments and passions. Murder is wrong because from the evidence of repeated experience it displeases. Yet within that subjective realm, as Hobbes had maintained, self-love was pre-eminent.

Smith, therefore, has to steer a course between rationalism and Hobbes. He can hardly deny the evidence that humans are self-interested, that self-love is a principle of human nature. Indeed his acceptance of it is a crucial element in the *Wealth of Nations*. Smith confronts this head on in the *Moral Sentiments*. Everyone, he declares, whether in a modern commercial society or not, has a 'natural preference . . . for his own happiness above that of other people' (*TMS* 82). But this is not a fixed or an unalterable fact. It is a weakness of the Hobbesian/Mandevillean view that it cannot take on board the evidence that the communicative signals sent via social interactions restrain selfish behaviour. The effect of the social mirror needs to be taken into account. In his elaboration of this effect Smith introduces another crucial notion.

The impartial spectator and conscience

Another of the facts that Smith attributes to human nature is that everyone wishes 'not only praise but praiseworthiness'. What this means is that humans apply standards to themselves. Of course, we like to be praised, because to be looked upon favourably by others is pleasing (I am elevated or emotionally uplifted by the public success of my poem). But we, also, want to deserve the praise we receive (the poem has not been plagiarized). More than that, we are pleased with having acted in a praiseworthy manner, even if nobody praises us. To capture the fact that we do not rely on actual praise or blame to do what we think we ought to do Smith introduces the notion of an 'impartial and well-informed spectator' (*TMS* 130). We seek to act in such a way that this fictional or imagined figure would approve of our conduct.

This spectator is an internalized standard or benchmark of what is right or wrong. In his description of this standard Smith frequently uses legal terminology but does so with a heavily rhetorical flourish. This spectator is described twice as 'the man within the breast, the great judge and arbiter' (*TMS* 130, 137). It is only by consulting this internal judge that we can evaluate our own actions or apply standards to ourselves.

As an 'inhabitant of the breast' the impartial spectator is explicitly identified by Smith with the principle of conscience. Perhaps I find a bag containing £1,000 but before handing it over to the police (and being publicly praised) I keep £100 for myself secure in the knowledge that no one will find out. But I feel guilty, my conscience tells me I should have returned the entire sum (I would then have been worthy of the praise). I judge myself by viewing my actions from the perspective of the impartial spectator, who being well informed knows my situation as well as whether my motives are self-serving.

Why should I pay any attention to that judgment? Smith's rhetoric suggests it binds me because it possesses some 'higher' authority. He refers three times to conscience as a 'demi-God within the breast' (*TMS* 131, 245, 247). He also refers to 'the all-wise Author of Nature' who created man as his 'vice-regent upon earth to superintend the behaviour of his brethren' (*TMS* 130). However, despite that Divine provision this superintendence, provided by what Smith calls 'the man without' (who praises or blames), gives way to the higher tribunal of conscience or 'the man within' (who assesses praiseworthiness or blameworthiness). Smith heavily amended these passages in the final edition and his own theological views are hard to determine.

On this question—to which there is no clear-cut answer—much hinges on how rhetorical these passages are taken to be. Are they merely literary or stylistic devices to make his argument seem familiar or persuasive to his readers, who are accustomed to seeing conscience as the word of God? Or, alternatively, are they to be taken at their face value as an expression of Smith's own beliefs? A similar ambivalence is raised by another passage. A few pages earlier Smith had referred to 'the all-seeing Judge of the world'. The context here is his observation that 'our' happiness in this life is often dependent on the 'humble hope and expectation of a life to come'. This hope he declares is 'deeply rooted in human nature' (*TMS* 131–2). This can be read as a neutral description, as a psychological fact. Smith himself observes that every religion (and superstition) provides support and comfort as well as a promise of reward and punishment in another life. It can also be read another way. The very depth of these roots means they are part of God's Design, humans were created with a soul and a belief in the afterlife.

But theological language does not monopolize Smith's discussion of conscience. On several occasions he refers to its authority as the effect of 'habit and experience' (*TMS* 135). To say it is habitual is to say it is a product of moral causation or is a learnt resource. From this perspective conscience has a social origin. This source and the recurrent references to learned experience once again sharply distinguish his account from Hutcheson. They also help to explain, or throw light on, the status of the impartial spectator.

This spectator is a product of the imagination. It reflects human powers and judgment not superhuman ones. The spectator is impartial not omnipotent. Moreover, human reflection upon experience is not fixed but changes as experience itself changes.

Even in one of passages where he invokes the 'great demigod', Smith refers to 'its' judgments as 'slow, gradual and progressive' (*TMS* 247). In that case, the inference is that they are not eternal or timeless moral commands like those entrusted to Moses.

This is consistent with Smith's recognition of historical change. In earlier ages what mattered was public standing. In later times what matters is conscience. Compare the cases of Achilles and Thomas More. The former was openly shamed by King Agamemnon taking his favourite slave. The latter would not compromise his principles to follow King Henry VIII's command. More followed his conscience, the 'man within'. Achilles left the battlefield because he had been humiliated before the 'man without'. Adopting the language of anthropologists, Smith has charted a shift from cultures where 'shame' is the source of moral discipline to cultures where guilt or conscience performs that role.

Relativism and moral judgment

The emphasis upon morality as something learnt seems to create another problem. It appears to equate ethical behaviour with social conformity; I approve what is customarily done in my own society. One solution to this apparent problem is provided by the impartial spectator. Not only can this figure be used by individuals to assess their own conduct, it can also be used to pass judgment on social institutions and policies.

Smith claims that everyone from observing both their own conduct and that of others can gradually form an idea of 'exact propriety and perfection' (*TMS* 247). In other words, we are all, though to varying degrees, able to establish an ideal or benchmark. This benchmark, in principle, enables us to assess whether our society is living up to its own standards and the extent, if any, to which current institutions or behaviours fall short. For example, Martin Luther King's 'I have a dream' speech in 1963 that everyone in the United States will be free one day is so powerful because, in the self-proclaimed 'land of the free', it juxtaposes that dream to the reality of the unfreedom of some.

Smith himself criticizes the court of the French king, Louis XIV. Louis' courtiers praise his limited talents and consequently cause the deprecation of the praiseworthy qualities or virtues of 'knowledge, industry, valour and beneficence'. This same scope for criticism could be applied closer to home. Smith is critical of several aspects of his own society. In practice, contemporary British politicians, he judged, instead of acting in the general interest, tend to favour special interests, like those of merchants who want to restrict trade. Again, in Book V of the *Wealth of Nations*, he expresses concern about the well-being in a civilized society of those who do repetitive, unstimulating (mind-numbing) work.

However, the initial problem seems to remain, it has only been pushed further down the road. The benchmark against which policies are judged appears to apply only within each society, each with its own standards. The impartial spectator is effectively an internalization of particular or local social experience. Smith appears to recognize this. He openly admits that what counts as virtuous conduct differs between 'rude and barbarous nations' and 'civilized nations' (*TMS* 205). But he does not accept that this confines all moral judgments to local circumstances, making morality socially specific or relative. On the contrary, he believes there are universal standards. For him, the moral sentiments of approval and disapproval have a solid foundation. They are founded on the 'strongest and most vigorous passions of human nature' (*TMS* 200). He allows that these passions may be warped or distorted but denies they can be completely overturned. Human passions provide a universal bedrock, on the basis of which universally valid judgments can be made. Regardless of time or place, no matter what the local circumstances, humans act and judge the same way on the same principles. There is a uniformity and constancy in human nature. Pleasure pleases and is pursued, pain is avoided. It is on that stable basis that Smith thinks it possible to establish a 'science of human nature' (*TMS* 319).

As an example of universal standards in operation he cites the practice of infanticide. There is evidence that in the earliest period of society infanticide was commonplace. Echoing the language of the 'Astronomy', Smith refers to 'we' not being in a state of 'wonder' or 'surprise' about this. The 'we' in question are the scientists of human nature (or social scientists) who, armed with the notion of moral causation, are able to explain both primitive infanticide and its persistence. In what he describes as the 'rudest and lowest state of society' humans live precariously, because resources are few and precious (*TMS* 210). Human nature being what it is (a scientific fact) in a condition of 'extreme indigence' an infant would be abandoned in order that the adult might live.

But though infanticide is in this way explicable, this does not make Smith a moral or social relativist. He does not subscribe to the view that to explain all is to pardon all. He acknowledges that infanticide in rude societies is more excusable than its occurrence 'among the polite and civilized Athenians'. In this latter case, where daily life is not so desperate, infanticide was inexcusable. Smith is adamant that just because something is commonly done does not exempt it from external criticism, when the practice itself is 'unjust and unreasonable'. According to Smith the Athenian practice of leaving their infants to perish in the wild was the inertial effect of habit. This is another case of moral causation. It was the Athenians' habitual acceptance of the practice that blinded them to this 'horrible abuse' (*TMS* 210). So powerful is this inertia, Smith implies, that even the most acute minds of the time, such as Plato and Aristotle, accepted it as normal. Infanticide is not an isolated case. The same argument applies to superstitions, slavery, and torture. Moral sentiments are ultimately rooted in some constants of human life. Although societies differ, and so moral judgments will also be subject to variation, this does not mean that all societies are morally equal. Smith is here reflecting a common Enlightenment position. Societies rife with superstition, suffering from mistaken beliefs, or pursuing self-destructive policies are all in their different ways ignorantly benighted and inferior to those where the light of knowledge shines. It is central to the agenda of the *Wealth of Nations* to demonstrate that this is the case.

Chapter 4
Living virtuously

Does someone deserve to be praised or punished? Can one individual merit owning more resources than another? Can blame be rightly attached to unintended actions? These are examples of moral questions that arise in everyday life. The *Moral Sentiments*, as the sub-title added to the third edition states, is an 'analysis of the principles' that govern or underlie judgments of human conduct and character. In line with that intent Smith needs to investigate the principles implicit in these types of questions, along with their answers. In his analysis he continues to use his account of sympathy.

Now the focus is not initially on the actor but on the recipient, or the 'object', of the action. If someone is the object of generosity from another, then we sympathize with the joy of the recipient and 'go along with' the gratitude to the benefactor. But if the gratitude is absent or grudging then the spectator will not sympathize with the recipient. Similarly, the spectator will sympathize with the distress of a victim of a burglary and also with the victim's appropriate feeling of anger and resentment toward the burglar. In the same way that feeling grateful is the natural response to an act of generosity, so feeling resentful is the natural response to an act of ill-treatment or injustice. The sentiment of resentment lies at the root of Smith's account of justice.

Justice

By locating the source of justice in the natural human sentiment of resentment, Smith differs from Hume. For Hume justice was not 'natural' in Smith's sense but a social practice or convention that was developed because it was useful. Justice had utility. It stabilized social arrangements, especially those regarding property (burglary destabilizes). Smith for his part is also emphatic that justice is important. It performs the necessary job of underpinning social order. However, he denies that this utility is the initial source of justice. According to Smith we sympathize with Betty whose flat has been burgled; she is the victim of an unjust act. It is the specific suffering of Betty that first concerns or animates us. This animation is generated without us paying any 'regard to the preservation of society' (*TMS* 89). Unlike Hume who put utility upfront, Smith thinks this is a subsequent development. On Smith's reading of human nature, humans 'delight' in seeing the unjust (Betty's burglar) punished. This delight is simply an effusive expression of the basic human disposition to resent injustice. Smith speculates that the sense of resentment appears to be rooted in our natural need to defend ourselves or to retaliate when harmed. What makes this an appropriate response is that the retaliation would get the approval of the 'impartial spectator'. Here lies the initial source of the virtue of justice.

The impartial spectator's approval is, however, conditional. It would be withheld if, for example, the impetus to retaliate was excessive and, if consequently, it started a cycle of violence and thus did more harm than good. This is where Smith gives reason its proper role. It formulates 'general maxims' (*TMS* 319). These are based on experience. They are derived from the evidence that human behaviour is not haphazard; there are recurrent or constant connections. For example, private vendettas or blood feuds should not be allowed to develop because they damage social cohesion. In formulating these maxims, reason is the source of 'the general rules of morality' (*TMS* 320). This links to justice because it consists in following rules.

Humans act justly by adhering to known rules and act unjustly by breaking them. Justice requires forbearance, not hurting another. It is, Smith says, a negative virtue. From this it consistently follows that 'we may often fulfil all the rules of justice by sitting still and doing nothing'. Smith admits this passive behaviour is not especially merit-worthy but that in no way detracts from its cardinal importance. Justice is indispensable. In another of his rhetorical set pieces, justice is the 'main pillar that upholds the whole edifice' so that if it was removed then human society would 'crumble into atoms' (*TMS* 86).

This holds in hard cases. A sentinel who falls asleep on his or her watch is justly executed for breaking the 'laws of war' even though the natural resentment felt at the offence would not by itself generate so severe a punishment. Although justice is necessary to all forms of society Smith thinks its rules are capable of improvement. He concludes the *Moral Sentiments* by contrasting the circumstances of early societies, where the system of justice is irregular (think of vendettas) with those in a 'more civilized nations', where the 'natural sentiments of justice' arrive at 'accuracy and precision' (*TMS* 341).

Those last two attributes are key elements. In their accuracy and precision the rules of justice are predictable or strict; either an action is legal or it is not and punishment reliably not randomly follows any infringement. These rules are not set in tablets of stone nor are they discovered by the intellect alone. They are, rather, the product of 'discipline, education, and example' (*TMS* 163). This is another way of saying that we are socialized into behaving justly. Thanks to this shared learning experience pretty much everyone can live decent, blameless lives. Social living does not require the extraordinary or super-human qualities possessed by saints or heroes. Individuals are able to live more or less peaceably together because they have been brought up to share a sense of justice. This sentimental agreement is a source of trust. It instils a mutual confidence that others can be relied upon. They will pay their debts, keep their promises, play their part in joint enterprises, and so on.

This confidence lays down the preconditions for a successful modern commercial society. A commercial society rests upon reliability. Its members need to be certain that obligations will be met, that contracts will be adhered to, and that transgressors will be punished. If the rules of justice are not strict, but variable, then this certainty is compromised. Without certainty and mutual confidence in the behaviour of others the division of labour, trade, and markets would not be viable. This is a crucial argument in the *Wealth of Nations*. In the *Moral Sentiments* Smith's example of the indispensability of justice is a society of merchants. He chose this example quite deliberately to identify a society where 'mutual love and affection' are absent (*TMS* 86). Those sentiments are not essential since buyers and sellers can coexist without any emotional attachments between them. Internet shopping illustrates the point.

Smith concedes that this society where love is absent is not very appealing. It will, however, be rule-abiding. By keeping the rules its members are acting justly, they will at a minimum follow the injunction 'not to injure another'. This forbearance is the mark of a 'perfectly innocent and just man' (*TMS* 218). It is not, however, the sole attribute. Smith additionally claims that this individual, in fact, will do more than merely follow the rules of justice, he will also revere them. Nor is this reverence an isolated trait. Smith believes it will be accompanied with many other virtues, like humanity and benevolence.

Benevolence

Despite these accompaniments, it remains the case that the indispensability of justice means that benevolence (generosity, charity, gratitude, etc.) is less essential to the existence of society than justice. There is nothing startling here. It was a commonplace feature of the jurisprudence that Smith taught. In that context a distinction was drawn between imperfect and perfect duties. Benevolence is an example of an imperfect duty, justice of a perfect duty. The significance of this distinction is that while you cannot be forced by law to be grateful or generous or kind or polite, you will be punished for burglary.

To act justly is negative. To act benevolently is positive, it is to do something. Benevolent actions are typically directed at those known personally to us. They reflect what Smith calls 'habitual sympathy' developed by the relatively permanent interactions within the family and between friends, co-workers, and fellow citizens (*TMS* 219). In those particular or localized arenas it is possible to do good deeds, but universal benevolence is not practical. In practice benevolence is exercised at our discretion and in a necessarily partial fashion. I will happily let my friend stay in my flat without any charge but would be reluctant to offer the same hospitality to a stranger.

By contrast, justice is not discretionary and is impartial. Our transactions with butchers (say) is payment for sausages; we do not in the normal course of events appeal to their benevolence or humanity but rather, says Smith in the *Wealth of Nations*, to their 'self-love' (*WN* 27). This, of course, is not to say that the butcher cannot be benevolent, she may give a beggar some sausages but that is at her discretion, whereas handing over the correct quantity of sausages for the correct payment is not.

By emphasizing the strict regularity of justice Smith is restricting its scope. This restriction has, he believes, an advantage over two other more expansive views or arguments. For Smith the advantage of his restricted view is that it more reliably achieves the key qualities of greater precision and certainty than the other two.

According to the first of these, justice encompasses all the virtues, so it is equally unjust not to admire a work of art as it is to neglect one's own welfare. This view is so expansive that it lacks any precision. According to the second argument we treat unjustly someone who deserves our charity or gratitude but we withhold it. From Smith's perspective, this view is still liable to introduce uncertainty. Perhaps Colin thinks it is just that public resources should go to providing for the homeless, but Yvonne thinks it is just that these resources should go to cancer patients. Though they disagree yet they are both using the language of justice to promote their choice. This makes an appeal to justice indeterminate and open to debate. However, both Colin and Yvonne will agree that it is just that burglars are punished. Justice here is not a matter for debate.

An efficient economy, Smith will argue in the *Wealth of Nations*, requires agreement, the confidence that burglars are punished. The uncertainty that comes from not knowing whether cancer treatment or affordable homes will be supported makes it more difficult to plan ahead. Should limited funds be committed to drug research or to bricks and mortar?

The 'invisible hand'

From the 20th century onwards, whether the homeless or cancer patients should get public resources is seen as a question of 'social' or 'distributive' justice. The underlying principle is that distribution should aim to achieve a 'fair' society. As a matter of social justice, buying a house should be affordable to those on low incomes and this can be made possible by justly redistributing some resources from those on high incomes. Smith does not in that sense have a theory of distributive justice but that absence does not make him exceptional in his own time.

What is more distinctive, without being unique, is that he thinks a deliberate policy to redistribute resources is not necessarily the best way to achieve the goal of greater material prosperity to the benefit of all. Smith's use of the metaphor of the 'invisible hand' illustrates this. He employs this metaphor three times. In the 'History of Astronomy' it refers to the actions of the gods. In the *Wealth of Nations* it refers to investment decisions, though he says there it applies in 'many other cases' (*WN* 456).

The third location is in the *Moral Sentiments*, where the metaphor crops up in the course of a complicated, knotty argument that needs unravelling. Humans, he declares, are motivated to strive or be industrious because they imagine themselves enjoying the 'pleasures of wealth and greatness'. The work and toil required to obtain this imagined state of happiness looks like a price worth paying. However, Smith describes this as a 'deception'. Unlike the neutral or descriptive role given to imagination in the theory of sympathy it now seems to characterize what is fanciful or wishful. In the context of this discussion the 'imagined' looks like the inferior opposite of what is 'real'. All this toil does not produce 'real happiness' or 'real satisfaction'. In reality, happiness is found in 'ease of body and peace of mind' and these are not the prerogative of the rich, even beggars can enjoy them. The 'baubles and trinkets' with which the rich surround themselves do not make their owners 'happy'.

The claim that mental tranquillity is the key to happiness has a long history. It is a central tenet of Stoicism and this philosophical outlook, originating in Greece and developed by the Romans, had many adherents in Smith's time. Smith, like all other 18th-century scholars, was familiar with this philosophy. According to the Stoics and their followers, we should only value what is under our control (such as peace of mind) and not invest value in riches or power which, because they can be lost or taken away, are outside our control. But Smith is no Stoic. He rejects this stark contrast between, on the one hand, rational self-control and living austerely and, on the other, enjoyment of material possessions and living in comfort.

This rejection follows from Smith's judgment that the deception has positive effects. The imagined, pleasurable lifestyle of the rich does indeed incentivize. The toil and industry thus stimulated has led to improvements in human life. The material conditions and moral circumstances of human life have been transformed. To depict this transformation, Smith indulges in another of his rhetorical set pieces. By means of this deception:

> Mankind…was first prompted to cultivate the ground, to build houses, to found cities and commonwealths, and to invent and improve all the sciences and arts, which ennoble and embellish human life; which have entirely changed the whole face of the globe, have turned the rude forest of nature into agreeable and fertile plains, and made the trackless and barren ocean a new fund of subsistence and the great high road of communication to the different nations of the earth. (*TMS* 183–4)

The implication is clear. If Stoic precepts had been adhered to and humankind confined themselves to supposedly 'real' satisfactions, then human life would have been crude and impoverished. For Smith there is nothing noble or commendable about poverty. It was because of their extreme indigence that savages felt compelled to let their children die. Underlining the key point, he later calls the cultivation of land together with the advancement of manufactures and increase of commerce, 'real' improvements that have benefited humankind and he reiterates the judgment that they have 'ennobled' human nature (*TMS* 229).

The *Wealth of Nations* tells the full story of this positive transformation—the move from miserable poverty to universal opulence—but the distributive aspect of these improvements is raised in the *Moral Sentiments*. The rich give employment to those who 'fit up' their palaces. They do not employ people out of a sense justice or compassion but because they desire those baubles and trinkets (Smith has no qualms about calling these desires 'vain and insatiable'). It is by pursuing their desires that the rich unintentionally advance the broader interest of society. And now (at last) Smith employs the metaphor: the rich 'are led by an invisible hand' to distribute 'necessaries of life' and this is as effective as an intended or deliberate distribution (*TMS* 184). With the growth and diffusion of opulence, these 'necessaries' can include housing and medicines.

Smith is now consistently able to argue that making distribution a direct or intentional object of justice is not necessary; his strict view can produce the same outcome. Of course, a number of background social conditions are needed for this to happen and these are identified and discussed in the *Wealth of Nations*. In the discussion of the invisible hand in the *Moral Sentiments* theological language briefly re-appears. The division on earth between the few 'lordly masters' and the many is the work of Providence (*TMS* 185).

But that is not the whole story. Providence has not abandoned the many because (thanks to the invisible hand) they get their share of goods produced. This is in line with a contemporary commonplace. Humans, with their limited understanding, should have faith that God in His wisdom has ordained an ultimately beneficial outcome. Smith, however, does not elaborate. He cites no biblical texts or commentaries neither here nor, some allusions aside, anywhere else in the book. That silence helps reinforce his analytical aim in the *Moral Sentiments*. But this is not all he has to say about the relation between the rich and the poor.

Ranks and corruption

How the rich and the poor relate to each other is another example of sympathy in action. Humans sympathize more with joy than sorrow. The reason Smith gives for this is that the depth and intensity of grief is more difficult to go along with than the delight expressed by the happy. He uses this to explain the observable social fact that the rich parade their wealth while the poor hide their poverty. As social creatures, humans get pleasure from the approval of others. This is principally why the rich value their wealth. It is less for the greater creature comforts that they can buy and more for the esteem or prestige their wealth attracts. They desire the admiration of others above their own personal enjoyment of their baubles.

This has direct social consequences. The desire to be admired lies behind a phrase that Smith employs both in the *Moral Sentiments* and several times in the *Wealth of Nations*. We all want 'to better our condition' (*TMS* 50; *WN* 99, 341, 343). We all want to be admired and the surest way to get that wish fulfilled is to be rich. In consequence, we work to improve our material circumstances and, in so doing, put ourselves into a position to receive admiration. This wish to be an object of admiration is a description of the way the (Smithian) world is, the evidence is that humans clearly do 'go along with the passions of the rich and powerful'. Smith's explanation for this fact is that it is a 'disposition of mankind' (*TMS* 52). People are disposed to admire others without expecting any benefit to come their way as a consequence.

It is this disposition, Smith now argues, that lies at the root of rank distinctions. The language of 'social class' had not yet been established. This fits the facts as Smith sees them. But this is also one of the places where he most openly deviates from his analytical or descriptive approach. In the expanded sixth edition, he inserts a new chapter directly after the one that discusses ranks. The title of this extra chapter is indicative: 'Of the corruption of our moral sentiments, which is occasioned by this disposition to admire the rich and the great, and to despise or neglect persons of poor and mean condition'. In this new chapter he still continues to assert the necessity of rank distinctions and, with them, social order. Indeed in another addition he re-affirms the place of ranks and emphasizes that the 'peace and order of society' is more important than 'the relief of the miserable' (*TMS* 226).

Yet even in this second passage Smith is judgmental. The rich and great are 'too often' preferred to the wise and virtuous. This contrast between the rich and the virtuous is the running theme in the added chapter. Both are subject to emulation. But those who want to emulate the wise and virtuous are, Smith laments, merely a select few. In contrast 'the great mob of mankind' are the 'worshippers' of wealth and greatness (*TMS* 62).

Although his choice of words reveals his own judgment he does not moralize; he does not seek to chastise or openly advocate a change in sentiments. Once again, he acknowledges experience. The evidence is that even when of equal merit most people will, in practice, respect the rich and the great more than the poor and humble. The evidence must be respected and moralistic hand-wringing will not change the facts.

In this chapter Smith goes on to introduce the circumstances and virtues of those in the 'middling and inferior stations of life'. He contrasts these individuals with those in 'superior stations'. He refers to a young nobleman whose chief aim is to cut a dash on the dance-floor and who is horrified at the possibility of having to exercise the virtues of knowledge, industry, patience, or self-denial. But these same virtues are those that the middle and inferior ranks possess. It is through their own efforts and abilities that they have bettered their condition and made their way in the world. With more than a hint of complacency, Smith endorses this meritocratic picture by remarking that in those ranks ability is generally rewarded with commensurate success—in most cases virtue and fortune happily coincide.

Without Smith openly saying so, this happy situation describes a commercial society and not one where the nobility sets the moral tone. This interpretation is backed up in the *Wealth of Nations* where he says of post-Union Scotland that 'the middling and inferior ranks' have escaped from the previously oppressive power of the aristocracy. These same passages also reveal that there is more to Smith's discussion of virtue than an analysis of justice and benevolence.

Prudence and other virtues

From the beginnings of Western moral philosophy in the teachings of Socrates, four 'cardinal' virtues were identified. The quartet comprised prudence, temperance, courage, and justice. Of all the virtues Smith declares that prudence is the one most useful to us. To be prudent is to pay attention to one's health, fortune, rank, and reputation. The impartial spectator approves of prudent conduct because it shows a willingness to sacrifice present advantage (e.g. spending my money now on a scooter) for greater return later (e.g. saving my money to buy a car). Although prudence, like justice, is not the 'most ennobling of virtues' it too fits the circumstances of a commercial society (*TMS* 216). In that society, the disposition or virtue of the prudent is to get on with their own affairs. They are not disposed to make waves or get involved in public service, let alone seek glory.

Prudence, like justice, is in this way especially suitable for life in a society where, as he puts in the *Wealth of Nations*, everyone is 'in some measure a merchant' (*WN* 37). The same can be said of the virtue of temperance, also called moderation or self-command. But commercial society recalibrates it. Compared to the more forgiving environment of family and friends, where sympathetic concord requires less negotiation, in the relatively anonymous setting of the market-place more effort is needed to negotiate the harmony or concord between actors and spectators. This extra effort has the effect of strengthening the character. In other words, the actor in a modern, commercial society exercises more moderation and exhibits more consistently the virtue of self-command than is possible in more tribal or clannish times. Feckless or reckless behaviour is more likely to be forgiven or tolerated among friends and family than it is from a 'faceless' institution like a bank, especially if you want to secure a loan.

Interacting with strangers instils self-discipline. Exuberant behaviour in the bar among friends would be out of place on public transport.

Smith refers to these effects of commercial living as 'gentler' exertions of self-command. You don't have to live an utterly joyless life to get a bank loan, just act with appropriate self-restraint. These milder exertions give 'lustre' to the distinctively commercial virtues of industry and frugality (*TMS* 242). Smith rebukes those who would disparage these virtues in favour of a harder or more severe regime. Again he has the Stoics in his sights. In addition he targets those he labels 'whining and melancholy moralists'. These moralists judge it wrong (impious even) to experience 'the natural joy of prosperity' when so many others are suffering from poverty and disease (*TMS* 139). One of the main arguments in the *Wealth of Nations* is to dispel that melancholic picture. In a properly organized commercial society the joy of prosperity is not confined to the wealthy, the poor too can have their share of enjoyment.

The link made by Smith between the commercial virtues and gentle self-command also connects to courage, the fourth cardinal virtue. Whereas the other three fit or are adaptable to commercial society, the same cannot be easily said of courage. It is out of step with modern life. In commercial society it is replaced with another more appropriate virtue. In Greek (*andreia*) and Latin (*virtus*), the words for courage and virtue have the same root as the word for male (*aner-andra/vir*). Literally to be brave (virile) was to act like a man. Gentleness, by contrast, was a feminine attribute. Smith does not question that being in command of one's fears is a virtue but he effectively replaces it with the virtue of 'humanity', which he defines as 'the virtue of a woman' (*TMS* 190).

Smith ties the expression of humane sentiments to a heightened sensitivity to the feelings of others. Humanity is a 'soft' virtue. Its presence in commercial society reflects social and moral development. There is a shift from hard to soft. The infanticide practised by 'savages' is a case in point but that is not an isolated example. Savage societies value, for example, the ability to resist torture but, according to Smith, this hardiness diminishes their humanity. Being able to withstand the pain of torture is not an exemplary demonstration of the virtues of self-command or courage. Nor is the Stoic indifference to bodily afflictions (retaining peace of mind even though in chains) any more commendable.

Even when Smith allows that command of fear and anger (as exhibited on the battlefield by the valiant or courageous) is 'great and noble' he qualifies it (*TMS* 241). He points out that when not at the service of justice and benevolence this attribute can be used to further injustice (great warriors like Genghis Khan slaughtered and enslaved entire populations). In contrast, the 'gentler exertions' of self-command rarely lead to bad consequences. Nor are these exertions to be judged inferior. The reverse is the case; it is in peaceable, civilized societies that these exertions have their home and correspondingly it is in those societies that both humanity and self-command are to be found. More than that, they are found to the highest degree.

This downplaying of courage relative to humanity, as hard gives way to soft, has another dimension. The savage is prone to 'falsehood and dissimulation' and the injustice to which valiant warriors are prone can also take the form of deceit (as when the wooden horse left by the Greeks was used to infiltrate Troy). In sharp contrast, a 'polished people' acquire habits that make them 'frank, open and sincere' (*TMS* 208). In his Glasgow lectures, Smith observed that probity and punctuality are 'the principal virtues of a commercial nation' (*LJ* 539). In line with the negotiated concord that lies at the heart of Smith's moral theory these principal virtues will reinforce each other. Honesty begets honesty: be trustworthy and you will be trusted. The outcome is regular conduct, mutual reliability, and confidence in the actions of others, which is precisely the hallmark of modern society.

It is a central plank in Smith's overall philosophy that individuals (merchants 'in some sense') in a commercial society are, in general terms, able to act justly, prudently, and benevolently. There is no divergence between the 'moral' and 'economic' aspects of his thought. The so-called 'Adam Smith Problem', first raised in the 19th century, according to which the role of 'sympathy' of the *Moral Sentiments* was at odds with the role of self-interest in the *Wealth of Nations* rests on a misreading of both texts. Smith's views on justice, prudence, and the 'joy of prosperity' developed in the *Moral Sentiments* are an integral part of the *Wealth of Nations*.

Chapter 5
Making and working

The *Wealth of Nations* is a big book. The definitive Glasgow edition has two volumes with over 900 pages in total. It was a long time in the making. Published in 1776 its roots can with certainty be traced back to Smith's lectures at Glasgow University in the 1750s. His thinking was subsequently shaped by his time in France, where he met several thinkers working on related themes. He also received practical information from merchants in Glasgow and landowners in Scotland. Thanks to the generous pension from the family of the Duke of Buccleuch, he was able on his return from France to focus on composing the book. This took several years which were largely spent with his mother in Kirkcaldy.

The *Wealth of Nations* is the most famous book in the history of economics because it was 'the father of modern economic thinking'. Its fame rests on it being the first systematic analysis of what Smith called 'commercial society' (the term 'capitalism' is a later coinage). There were plenty of other books before Smith's that discussed the subjects he would cover. Many of these were pamphlets or books written to argue a particular case, such as a defence of trading companies like the East India Company or to support the balance of trade and the interests of merchants. There were others which, like the *Wealth of Nations*, did develop a general and more theoretical approach, and scholars have traced Smith's indebtedness to some of these. Smith himself is sparing in his references to other works (he makes an exception in referring to the work of Hume), but it is fair to say that none of these discussions had the range or depth of Smith's book. Hume wrote suggestive essays and Richard Cantillon, perhaps his most analytically sophisticated predecessor, unlike Smith, did not situate his analysis in a broad historical and social context.

The organization of the *Wealth of Nations*

Although systematic the book is complicated. It contains a number of what Smith explicitly calls 'digressions'. One of these (on the value of silver) runs to seventy pages. The book also addresses some immediate contemporary issues, most notably the increasingly fraught relation ship between Britain and the American colonies. The *Wealth of Nations* comprises five books, divided into chapters, some of which are then sub-divided into parts. There is a very brief Introduction. This brevity is helpful because it highlights what Smith himself judged to be key points.

Book I discusses the role and extent of the division of labour (what he calls in the Introduction, the productive powers of labour) and how the products of labour are distributed among the different sectors or ranks of society. In his summary of this book, Smith makes a point of contrasting the dire conditions of life in 'savage nations' with those in 'civilized and thriving nations' (*WN* 10). That contrast is a key theme that runs throughout the *Wealth of Nations*. It lies at the heart of his conviction that a commercial society is superior to earlier forms of social life.

Book II examines 'stock' or capital. It discusses how stock is accumulated and the different ways it is put to use. In the course of this discussion Smith distinguishes between unproductive and productive or useful labour. This is not a moral distinction, implying that the latter is better than the former. On his own criterion Smith himself as a professor or author is unproductive. Unlike the manufacturer (e.g. a pin-maker) who makes an enduring product from given materials (pins from metal) and thus creates capital that can be re-invested to promote economic growth (to make more—and better—pins), the author of the *Wealth of Nations* produces or generates nothing that is similarly 'productive'.

Book III reproduces more obviously the content of some of his Glasgow lectures. Its focus is more historical. It outlines how the feudal system of land tenure and the social and political power that ownership gave to the landowners was gradually replaced by a commercial society. This replacement illustrates a procession of unintended consequences, a central thread in the *Wealth of Nations* and throughout Smith's work.

Book IV is largely polemical. Smith takes aim at what he sees as the chief rival to the account he is providing. He calls this rival the mercantile system. This system aimed to regulate the economy on the principle that exports should be increased but imports restricted. The wealth of a nation consisted in a monetary surplus and benefited producers not consumers. But for Smith the wealth of nations lies in the productivity of labour and the better living standards that generates; an outcome that is best achieved by free trade. One of the reasons why the *Wealth of Nations* is such a big book is that Smith is not dogmatic. His reasoning is nuanced and his arguments frequently qualified, so his defence of free trade, for example, allows for exceptions.

Book V is the longest. It focuses on sources of revenue and expense. The latter of these deals with the maintenance of socially necessary tasks, like government and education, but which are unproductive in Smith's technical sense. The former examines how these tasks are to be funded or what are effective means to raise income from tax. This leads to the last topic. Revenue can also be gained by government borrowing or incurring public debt but, as he points out, it is an unintended consequence of this method that it can make matters worse.

Stages and the pre-history of a commercial society

As an educated man in the 18th century Smith had been schooled in the classics of Greek and Roman literature. He also got information from the reports of missionaries and voyagers on societies in the Americas, Asia, and more recently Polynesia that are very different to his own. There were, however, similarities between the accounts of the Iroquois provided by Father Lafitau in the early 18th century and of the German tribes provided by the 1st-century CE historian Tacitus (both writers are cited by Smith). But 18th-century Hesse is very different from the settlement of the Batavi in that location, while in Smith's time Glasgow was not that dissimilar to Antwerp. From this stock of knowledge two conclusions were drawn. Commercial society was only one type of society and it was modern. This enabled Smith, and other Enlightenment thinkers, especially his fellow Scots, to differentiate societies historically. Some forms of social life could be understood as more advanced than others.

In his lectures on jurisprudence delivered in Glasgow, Smith identified four types of society in a rough historical sequence, developing through hunter, shepherd, agricultural, and commercial stages. His context was the development of property rights. This notion of stages was a teaching tool. It was a way of bringing out to his students how differing social situations generate different forms of ownership and different modes of regulation. The first three of these four types all revolve around the dominant mode of subsistence and were identified by many other writers. It is Smith's explicit reference to a 'commercial society' that is distinctive and Smith here is a pioneer. The *Wealth of Nations* is the systematic investigation of this society. Although the 'four stages' does not figure prominently in the book the fact that he sees commercial society as a historically distinctive type remains an important backdrop.

In the second of the four stages the leaders are those who own
the greatest herds and similarly in the third agricultural stage
power lies with the owners of land. Smith is very clear that the
power held by the owners is exercised by them to protect their
own interests. In his Glasgow lectures he is blunt: government
in those stages is not neutral because in practice it is 'a
combination of the rich to oppress the poor' (*LJ* 208). This bias,
however, does not apply in the age of commerce. In that age,
governance is subject to the impersonal rule of law and not the
personal (despotic) rule of khans or feudal lords. He also made
this point in the 1790 edition of the *Theory of Moral Sentiments*,
where he writes that 'in commercial countries' the 'authority of
the law is sufficient to protect the meanest [i.e. poorest] man in
the state' (*TMS* 223).

The feudal lords were masters of their own local territory. They
settled disputes, enforced discipline, and commanded their
tenants to fight on their behalf. They could do this because they
owned the land on which those they commanded depend for their
livelihood. The tenants could only grow and retain for themselves
some of the crops if they did the lord's bidding. However, this
changed when foreign commerce introduced luxury goods.
To obtain what Smith deliberately calls frivolous and useless goods
(he mentions diamond buckles) the lords sold off their land or
granted long leases. The effect of this was to undermine their
power to command and their ability to act as judges because
those who had been previously dependent became independent.
As Smith vividly depicts this transition, it was 'for the gratification
of the most childish, the meanest and the most sordid of all
vanities' that these landlords gradually bartered away their
whole power and authority (*WN* 419).

Smith calls this change a 'revolution of the greatest importance to
the publick happiness' (*WN* 422). But it was not brought about
with the deliberate aim to further the public good but was, rather,

an example of unintended consequences. Everyone involved was out to get something for themselves. The landlords wanted the buckles for their own enjoyment and the merchants who supplied the buckles did so to make a living from retail and those tenants who stayed on the land (rather than moving into towns to trade) did so because they could then reap for themselves the full benefits of their labours.

This revolution was important because it made possible the 'regular administration of justice'. No longer was there a patchwork of local jurisdictions but the emergence (gradually) of a uniform system of law. The establishment of that uniformity is crucial; without it a commercial society is not possible. The *Wealth of Nations* is a scientific enquiry into the nature and causes (as the full title of the book states) of that society. Yet unlike most present-day economics, Smith's enquiry is sensitive to the fact that the subject of his analysis is a product of history.

The division of labour

For Smith a developed commercial society enjoys a 'universal opulence which extends itself to the lowest ranks of the people' (*WN* 22). It is the breadth of this opulence, by which Smith means not just riches or wealth but purchasing power, that is significant. Other societies have been opulent but this opulence was confined to their upper classes. It is a distinctive mark of commercial societies that the lower ranks are able not only to meet their basic needs but also able to enjoy a better quality of life. In a pointed conclusion to the book's opening chapter, Smith declares the quality of the accommodation of these ranks exceeds that of 'many an African king' (*WN* 24). Moreover, in a commercial society there are sufficient resources to care for the vulnerable—infanticide is no longer a decision imposed by extreme poverty. A central task of the *Wealth of Nations* is to explain this shift, to provide an account of economic growth or development that, in doing so, also accounts for the increase in well-being, or welfare, both socially and individually.

This diffused opulence does not occur in a social vacuum, it is only possible in a 'well-governed society'. The *Wealth of Nations* is not simply a work of economic analysis it is also a work that provides a political philosophy. This twin feature is neatly captured in a phrase from his Glasgow lectures when he tells his students that 'opulence and freedom are the two greatest blessings man can possess' (*LJ* 185).

The root cause of universal opulence is the division of labour. Smith thinks the source of this specialization of tasks is a 'propensity', an inclination or disposition, in human nature to 'truck, barter and exchange' (*WN* 25). He just asserts that humans possess this disposition, although he speculates that it is probably a consequence of the faculties of reason and speech. Earlier in his Glasgow classroom he tied the trucking disposition to the 'natural inclination to persuade' (*LJ* 352) which in the *Moral Sentiments* he labelled one of the strongest of human desires. As a further testimony to the connections across Smith's work, in the *Considerations* he had located the origin of language in the utterances of savages as they attempted 'to make their mutual wants intelligible to each other' (*CL* 203).

Because the division of labour is a propensity of human nature then it is true of everyone. It cannot, it follows, be an exclusive feature of commercial society. It exists throughout the four stages. With implicit reference to the first stage, Smith gives the example of a skilled bowmaker who discovers that by exchanging high-quality bows for the meat from deer slain by more adept hunters, he can obtain more venison than from trying to kill his own beast. This division is rudimentary because before the age of commerce there is little scope for extensive exchange. Why that is true of the earliest stages and untrue of the fourth stage hinges on the security generated by the rule of law, the definitive characteristic of a well-governed society.

Smith illustrates how an extensive division of labour produces opulence with the famous example of pin-making, a 'very trifling manufacture' as he calls it (*WN* 14). The example was often used and chosen by Smith precisely because it was familiar. He calculates that through the division of labour ten individuals could make 48,000 pins a day—equivalent to 4,800 each. But if each individual performed all the tasks required (drawing, straightening, cutting, pointing the wire, and so on) then less than twenty would have been manufactured. He gives three reasons for this: increased dexterity that comes from reducing each individual's task to 'one simple operation'; time-saving that stems from not having to transfer from one task to the next; and inventing better ways of executing the task prompted by the concentration on one task (*WN* 17). There is a downside to this specialization that Smith returns to later in his book.

The division of labour in this illustrative way increases the 'productive powers of labour' and is the engine of economic growth. But this is not an independent process. Its extensiveness, the key to its provision of opulence (a multitude of cheap pins), is dependent on the size of the market. When the population is small and scattered the scope for an extensive market is small. In these circumstances there is no incentive to specialize so as to produce a surplus to exchange for the surplus of another specialist; the propensity to exchange will remain largely dormant. Smith uses the Highlands of Scotland to illustrate how individuals are there forced to perform for themselves many tasks, 'every farmer' must be his own 'butcher, baker and brewer' (*WN* 31).

This example picks up one of the best-known passages in the *Wealth of Nations*, it is not from the benevolence of the butcher, the brewer or the baker that we expect our dinner, but from their regard to their own interest. We address ourselves not to their humanity but to their self-love and never talk to them of our own necessities but of their advantages. Nobody but a beggar chuses to depend chiefly upon the benevolence of his fellow-citizens. (*WN* 27)

I give the butcher money, she gives me sausages. This is not a claim that humans are exclusively motivated by self-love. The whole argument of the *Moral Sentiments* was to reject that claim. The butcher could well act benevolently and give some meat to the beggar but that could only be an occasional gesture because she would not stay in business long if she gave away her products. Nor is it a claim that humans are motivated simply to satisfy their basic needs. As he put it in his lectures, humans work to procure not just food, clothing, and accommodation but also 'conveniences' according to the 'nicety and delicacy' of their taste as well as to become objects of admiration (*LJ* 488). This is part of what makes us human. As the (now) cliché has it, man does not live by bread alone.

When bakery is a separate enterprise from brewing or butchery, when, that is, labour is more specialized, then the more necessary markets become. I will only specialize in bakery if I can reasonably expect others to be specializing in the production of other foodstuffs, so that when I take my bread to market I can, via the medium of money, exchange it for the produce of others. The decision to specialize depends on having confidence in a stable or predictable future. The butcher can rely on the baker for bread; the baker on the butcher for meat.

That reliance or confidence needs to be underwritten. This comes to be a central plank of Smith's account of the role of government as it upholds a system of justice. When the actions of others are not predictable then it is prudent to be independent and self-sufficient and not rely on anyone else. Everyone produces all their own food. But, of course, that option means forgoing the blessing of the opulence—poorer diet in this case—that comes from interdependence (the Highlands were far less prosperous than Glasgow).

Smith illustrates the interdependency of the members of a commercial society with the example of a coarse woollen coat. Even this humble product, he remarks, involves many thousands in its manufacture, from those involved directly to those indirectly, such as the makers of the tools used by the coat manufacturers. So extensive is interdependence that 'everyman thus lives by exchanging or becomes in some measure a merchant'. And when this has happened then this is 'properly a commercial society' (*WN* 37).

From this general basis Smith proceeds to more detailed technical discussions. These it has to be said are not always as clear or as consistent as they might be. He distinguishes, for example, four types of price and different roles played by labour.

Labour, price, and value

The opening sentence of the *Wealth of Nations* proclaims the importance of labour. The 'necessaries and conveniences of life' are obtained through it either directly or indirectly. It is direct when I bake the bread I consume and it is indirect when I buy a loaf, which is to say I purchase the labour of a baker. But interdependency means the baker would have to have bought flour from the labour of a miller and bought an oven from the labour of a manufacturer. The buying and selling of the products of labour requires a market and that requires some mechanism to calculate how much the bread, wheat, and oven should cost. This leads Smith into tricky questions of money, price, and value.

Smith describes money as 'the great wheel of circulation, the great instrument of commerce' (*WN* 291). Beyond the immediate barter of venison for a bow it is necessary to have some standard to enable the butcher, baker, and brewer to trade. He gives a long list of commodities that have acted as a standard—cattle, shells, sugar, and so on. But he says there was convergence on metals because they didn't perish and could be divided. In a commercial society, paper money gradually substitutes for gold and silver—a development that, later in the book, leads Smith into a discussion of banking and credit.

But money is only an instrument, a tool. It is a separate question how much a consumer pays for bread, beef, beer (and ovens). This raises what historically has been one of the most persistent problems in economics—the relation between price and value. Some objects have 'value in use'. Water is an example. Other objects have 'value in exchange'. Diamonds are an example. Smith observes that though water has the greatest use value it has no exchangeable value (you can't get much for it), while the opposite is the case with diamonds (you can get a lot in exchange for them). Though the distinction is important (it is a pivotal feature of Karl Marx's economics, for example) Smith is concerned with the 'principles that regulate the exchangeable value of commodities' (WN 46). Why is the price of a loaf £1 and a pint of beer £2?

Typically he starts with a simple almost intuitive observation and then unfolds a more elaborate analysis. He supposes in the hunter stage that it takes twice the labour to kill a beaver than it does a deer, so one beaver should exchange for two deer. This is their 'exchangeable value' and, in this simple situation, it is calculated by how much labour was expended (or embodied) in production. Labour is the real measure of exchangeable value and this constitutes the 'real price' of a commodity. It is distinct from the 'nominal price' or the sum of money paid (£1 for a loaf). While labour always remains the ultimate determinate, Smith continues to refine his analysis as the situation becomes more complicated than that portrayed by the deer/beaver example. When I buy rather than bake the loaf I am, in effect, 'commanding' the labour of the baker and this incorporates the labour he has, in turn, commanded from the miller and oven manufacturer.

He proceeds to identify three components in labour. It measures not only how much toil or effort is involved in baking but also measures the value of the land that grows the wheat and the cost in manufacturing and distributing the ovens to bake the bread. These three components of labour have their own local going rate and together they establish the bread's 'natural price' (*WN* 72). Across all marketable commodities this price is decided by what is sufficient to pay the rent, the wages, and the profits of 'the stock employed in raising, preparing and bringing' a good to market. They are in contemporary terminology the 'costs of production'.

Smith is now describing not a primitive society of hunters but a developed society where everyone 'in some measure' is a merchant. But even before such a society develops, labour as a unit of measurement is difficult to gauge. Money makes matters easier. The quantity of money (how much to pay) is a simpler measure than quantity (how much) and quality (skill) of labour. However, that simplicity means it is liable to fluctuate. For example, gold or silver can be more or less available, harvests more or less bountiful, workers more or less plentiful, but, more generally, the 'higgling and bargaining of the market' produces a going rate or the 'market price' (*WN* 49).

He illustrates the fluctuation in the market price with the example of a public mourning. In this situation the sudden increase in demand raises the price of black cloth because the quantity available is now in relatively short supply. Smith in this way identifies one of the lynchpins of modern 'neo-classical' economics, that price is set by the relation between supply and demand. But, thanks to these fluctuations, for him, the market price remains analytically distinct from the natural price.

They might coincide but the market price can also be above or below the natural price. For this reason Marx called him a representative of 'classical political economy' (indeed, along with David Ricardo, he was 'the best').

According to Smith's analysis, the market price, because it is always subject to fluctuations, does not really explain why bread costs £1 a loaf and beer £2 a pint. The explanation lies in the natural price. Smith uses a revealing metaphor. He says the natural price is that 'to which the prices of all commodities are continually gravitating' (*WN* 75). What is revelatory is the use of the Newtonian image of 'gravity' and Smith's implicit claim that he has scientifically explained the workings of the economy as Newton had done of the universe.

To his own mind he has uncovered the regulatory principles of exchange. If there is a shortfall between demand and supply then it is, where applicable, in the interest of landlords, labourers, and manufacturer to fill the gap by increasing supply. This activity is the gravitational pull and it will operate when the landlords and the others are free from artificial restrictions. As it is now called, this is a process of equilibrium. Smith's achievement is to have shown that the operation of the market has regularities or constantly recurring patterns; it is not a random haphazard series of interactions. This is more than sufficient for neo-classical economists to label him the 'father' of the discipline.

Labour, land, and stock comprise the three components of the natural price. In the form of wages, rent, and profit this provides Smith with a basic three-fold division of sources of income.

Wages

Before land became private property and before stock was accumulated, labourers enjoyed the whole produce of their labour. With the emergence of landlords and stockholders the labourers cannot act independently but must rely for their maintenance on the landlord or later, as society develops, from the manufacturer in the form of wages. Labourers must work on the privately owned land and landlords take their share of the labourers' product as rent. The pin-makers must be provided with the materials to make the pins, as well as wages (money to live on while making the pins). When the pins are sold the manufacturers reclaim their share as profit.

The psychology of the butcher and baker still applies. All three parties—labourers, landlords, and manufacturers—are motivated by their own interests. These, however, do not coincide. Smith observes that the labourers desire to get as much and the 'masters' (landlords, manufacturers) to give as little as possible. In pursuing their side of the contract labourers are disposed of their own accord to join forces or 'combine' in order to raise their wages, while the masters on their side combine to lower them. Smith now adds that the latter can combine more easily than the former, especially since the law prohibits the combination of workers, while permitting that of the masters. This leads Smith to make the forthright comment that 'masters are always and everywhere in a sort of tacit, but constant and uniform combination not to raise the wages above their actual rate' (*WN* 84).

This rate has a necessary floor. The wages paid must at least enable the labourer to subsist and bring up a family. This minimal level is what employers wish to pay. But that aim, Smith judges, reflects a misunderstanding. Many economists of his time, and earlier, took the view that low wages were a necessary incentive but Smith, on the contrary, argued in favour of high wages because, in one of his key phrases, and one he had already used in the *Moral Sentiments*, high wages encourage in the worker the hope of 'bettering his condition' (*WN* 99). The more the labourer is encouraged then the greater the productivity. This explains why wages are highest in times of economic growth. This supports one of Smith's major arguments. The central issue is not the monetary level of wages but their purchasing power: what those wages can buy. The purpose of production is consumption. This self-evident 'maxim', as he calls it, is the most important in the whole book. The wealth of nations lies in the increase of revenue and stock, in the availability and accessibility of more, better, and affordable goods.

Smith the economist is the same man as Smith the moral philosopher, and in the context of wages this is apparent. It is a matter of 'equity' that those who provide for the basic needs of society should themselves be 'tolerably well-fed, cloathed and lodged'. And since, as he said in the *Theory of Moral Sentiments*, prosperity brings joy, then 'no society can be flourishing and happy of which the greater part are poor and miserable' (*WN* 96). A similar moral tone recurs when Smith discusses merchants and manufacturers. They are hypocrites who complain about the effects of high wages but are silent about the bad effects of high profits and the 'pernicious effects of their own gains' (*WN* 115). Furthermore, they are deceitful and, because they always seeking to reduce competition, they are, in effect, conspiring against the public interest.

Profits

Smith has no objection to profits. They accrue from stock, which, when put to use, has the vital role of generating most of a society's useful labour. This role is the subject matter of the whole of Book II. It is a consequence of the division of labour that the pin-maker cannot make pins without the equipment to do so and has to have funds to live on before the pins are sold. The availability of this equipment and the resources to maintain the pin-maker are derived from existing stock. It follows that this stock must have been accumulated in advance. The greater the accumulation then the better the equipment that can be afforded and the higher the

incentivizing wages that can earned/paid which leads to greater
productivity and thus economic growth and greater national wealth.

Labourers possess little stock of their own and have scant
opportunity to accumulate. But if a quantity is built up then
stock-holders, after deducting what is needed for immediate
personal consumption, and in order to better their condition, will
aim to derive a revenue from the residue. They would, Smith says,
be 'perfectly crazy' if they didn't (*WN* 285). Smith here introduces
the term 'capital' and its accumulation is the key to growth.

Smith distinguishes two types of capital. The stock-holders can,
in broad terms, put their residual stock to work in two ways.
These are not mutually exclusive. They can manufacture goods
and then sell them for a profit, the proceeds of which are usable
to purchase more materials, etc., for more manufacture. Smith
calls this 'circulating capital' since it involves a series of exchanges
(*WN* 279). Or, second, the stock-holder can use the residue to
improve land or to buy machinery. This Smith labels 'fixed
capital' because once invested there is no further exchange
(*WN* 282). The aim of fixed capital, through these means, is to
increase the productivity of labour. The relative proportions
between these two types of capital will depend on the
stockholder's business, so more fixed capital (machinery) is
needed for mining coal than for making shoes. But the fixed
capital in mining or cobbling cannot of itself raise any revenue
without circulating capital to supply and maintain the pumps for
the mine or the leather for the shoe-maker as well as the upkeep
of the workers.

Capital will only be put to work, and economic growth ensue, if
there is 'tolerable security' (*WN* 285). Here is a persistent thread
in the *Wealth of Nations*. In the earlier ages when that security is
missing individuals will keep what stock they have close at hand.
They would be sane not crazy to keep hold of it. The result is no
investment which consequently limits the productivity of labour.

The effect of this is to entrench an impoverished life in comparison to that enjoyed even by humble labourers in a commercial society. The security afforded to all in that society makes it a safe and sane decision to invest. That security as well as promoting investment also facilitates wider and more intensive markets. A bigger market means more competition and that in its turn also leads to improvement both materially and socially.

This growth in productivity and overall prosperity makes it possible to sustain unproductive labour. Some of this labour is functional, including those whose job it is to maintain security, both internally and externally, and some of it is 'frivolous', including not only musicians but also the professions of the church, law, and medicine. The 'wealth' of nations also encompasses learning and culture.

Rent

In the same way that it is in the interest of an employer to pay wages at the lowest feasible level, so it is in the interest of a landlord to charge as much rent as the tenant can afford. But the cases are not identical. Not all rent takes the form of a reasonable profit from investment in improvement. The difference is that rent can still be derived from unimproved property. With explicit reference to Scotland, Smith gives the example of kelp. This seaweed is useful for making soap and glass but the raw product is not the result of any human industry. Nonetheless the owner of the shore demands a rent from the kelp harvester.

More rent can be charged for fertile than for less fertile land but, where fertility is equal, another factor is relevant. A higher rent can be charged on land that is close to the market town. The explanation for this is that the greater the proximity then the less the transportation costs in taking goods to the market, with the consequence that the income of these tenants is greater, making it feasible for the landlord to raise their rent. That differential would be reduced if transportation costs were also reduced and that would in its turn encourage the cultivation of land further away from the towns. This encouragement is beneficial because it facilitates the emergence of new producers to compete with the more locally based ones. It is because it stimulates this increased competition (always a 'good thing' for Smith) that he judges a developed infrastructure of good roads and canals to be the greatest of all improvements.

Social orders

Wages, profit, and rent as the three sources of income establish within a 'civilized society' three corresponding 'orders of people'—workers, merchants, or manufacturers and rentiers/ farmers. Although each is equally a component of society their relationship to the public or general interest differs. This difference matters when it comes to policy-making. Smith finds each order deficient when it comes to good governance.

The interests of those who live by wages are closely bound up with the general social interest, because as society prospers so do they and vice versa. However, their everyday circumstances mean they are relatively uneducated thus making them 'unfit' to inform policy (Smith returns to this deficiency in Book V). The second order—the 'country gentlemen' who live off rent—are the traditional mainstay of the political order and, as Smith acknowledges, because land as a natural resource is a fixed asset then their own interests in maintaining it will not run counter to those of the nation. But they are indolent and incapable of applying themselves to understanding the consequences of any public regulation. This scepticism of the link between landowning and political judgment reflects a remark in his Glasgow jurisprudence lectures that in a 'polished' or commercial society what counts is 'superior mental capacity' (*LJ* 401).

The final order, those whose income derives from profit, are more educated than the first and more intellectually active than the second. However, their interests and the general interest do not coincide, because the rate of profit, unlike wages and rent, does not necessarily harmonize with the prosperity of the country. Indeed, Smith claims the rate is highest in 'countries which are fast going to ruin'. This lack of harmony has bad consequences when it comes to policy-making. Smith proceeds to develop a prolonged critique of the policies typically advocated by merchants.

Chapter 6
Trading and spending

In Book IV of the *Wealth of Nations* Smith identifies two faulty alternatives to his own explanation of the wealth of nations. He criticizes the French economists (the Physiocrats) some of whom he met on his travels as a tutor. Their basic argument was that land is the sole source of wealth and revenue, but Smith, while agreeing with them on the importance of liberty, criticizes them for treating manufacturers and merchants as totally unproductive. However, Smith's chief target is the second alternative. This he calls the 'mercantile system'.

The critique of mercantilist politics

The core objective of the mercantile system was to achieve a favourable balance of trade (measured in bullion). This balance was to be achieved by encouraging a surplus of exports over imports. The latter were subject to high duties on goods that could be produced by domestic industry. By reducing competition, this policy is in the interests of home industry which is the same as saying it is in the interest of domestic manufacturers and merchants. To protect that interest they oppose any law that would threaten their control of the market. According to Smith, so powerful is this interest that it can intimidate the legislature (largely the mentally indolent landowners). This is made easier by the parliamentarians' belief that by accepting the merchants' arguments they gain a reputation for understanding trade as well as by them hoping to curry favour with the increasingly wealthy mercantile order.

Smith has a generally low opinion of politicians. Those who participate 'in the management of publick affairs' do so because of the prestige it gives them. They are not motivated by a commitment to public virtue. Not only are they swayed by outside interests but also they typically take the short view. Their skill he likens to an 'insidious and crafty animal'. He contrasts this opportunistic talent to 'the science of a legislator' that deals with invariable 'general principles' (*WN* 468). He had used this same term at the beginning of Book IV where he identifies 'political economy' as a branch of that science, the purpose of which is two-fold: to enable individuals to live well from their own efforts and to raise revenue. However, it is clear Smith is not advocating that some individual could play the role of 'legislator'. His emphasis is on the 'science' which his book is outlining.

Smith has more faith in the legal system than in politics. The replacement of the arbitrary localized judicial role played by the feudal lords by an independent judiciary is he declares in one of his Glasgow lectures the 'great advantage which modern times have over antient' (*LRBL* 176). He believes this independence makes it very unlikely that justice will be sacrificed to political expediency. This belief rests on two assumptions. He assumes judges are exceptionally able (unlike the bulk of the parliamentarians). He also assumes that, because their emolument is very small, they are motivated by the great honour of their office so that they treat the public admiration that comes with the job as 'part of their reward' (*WN* 123). This view, exemplified also in doctors, poets, and philosophers, incidentally, underlines the fact that Smith did not reduce all motivations to material self-interest.

Smith does not tar all politicians with the same brush. He allows for exceptions. There are in parliament some public-spirited individuals who object to or resist the mercantile lobby. But for their pains they are subject to abuse, insults, and even violence. This, for Smith, is all part of the 'mean and malignant' character of the mercantile system, as its supporters conspire to 'deceive, and even to oppress the publick' (*WN* 267).

These barbs reflect the effects, and are the corollaries, of mercantilism. But Smith's objections run deeper. The very aim of that system is misconceived because it elevates the interests of producers above consumers. Consumers benefit not from mercantile restrictions but from free trade. There are two aspects to Smith's deeper critique. He shows how mercantile policies in practice thwart the wealth of nations and he also demonstrates how in principle its assumptions are faulty and necessarily run counter to what he calls 'natural liberty'. This combination of practical and theoretical aspects reveals the core of his own system.

Free trade

According to Smith mercantilist policy seeks to 'force' trade into a particular direction (*WN* 506). His use of the word 'force' here helps to sharpen the contrast to his own policy of 'free' trade. The outcome of this forced attempt is worse than if the trade had been left to find its own way. The whole idea of a 'balance' of trade, to be achieved by artificially diverting industry away from its own course, is 'absurd' (*WN* 458). To illustrate this absurdity Smith gives a local example. With the help of artificial devices, like greenhouses, good wine, he says, can be produced in Scotland. But the production of Scottish wine would require so much capital that, compared to importing wine from France, it would be expensive. As a result, it would, he judges, be unreasonable to prohibit the import of cheaper claret.

This deliberately contrived example, dramatizes three fundamental Smithian principles. The natural advantages of one country in producing some commodities (wine in France) make it wasteful to offset them in another (subsidize Scottish vineyards). The free trade in wine benefits the Scottish consumer, who pays less for his or her tipple; the subsidies would only benefit the owners of Scottish vineyards. Second, no regulation, like imposing bounties or subsidies, can increase the quantity of industry in a society beyond what its capital can sustain; it can only direct it. But, third, this will be a misdirection.

If a good is only produced because it is subsidized it means the producer would otherwise not engage in its production, since no profit would be earned. This entrenches inefficiency to the overall detriment of the economy. If there were no subsidies then a producer would not waste her capital in Scottish grape production but use it in an area where she can expect a reasonable return on the investment (say whisky). That expectation will be fulfilled if the good now produced has a market, that is, consumers who want whisky.

There is, though, no guarantee that a producer will be successful. This is because that same expectation would be shared by other producers who would use their capital to enter that same market and compete for the consumers' custom by also producing whisky (the same applies for wine production in France). In this way, thanks to free trade and competition, Scottish and French customers will be the ultimate beneficiaries, enjoying both cheaper wine and cheaper whisky. Not only will the drinks be cheaper but they will also be of better quality. In addition there will be more choice since the producers will compete to offer a drink that will 'give them an edge' in the market-place—*vin ordinaire* or *premier cru* of various vintages; blend or malt of varying age.

Smith supplies many other non-contrived examples, with particular attention paid to corn. He devotes one of his 'digressions' of almost twenty pages to it. In his treatment of this issue Smith was contributing to an intense contemporary debate and his 'take' caused much controversy both at the time and later. He used this topic to reinforce his argument about free trade and demonstrate that regulation was misplaced.

Left to his own judgment and in pursuit of his own interest, the corn dealer would set the price as high as the quantity of corn allows. When there is a shortage a high price will be charged. Contrary to the view that this is exploitative, Smith maintains this is to everyone's benefit. The high price will discourage over-consumption and encourage 'thrift and good management'. In that way adequate supply will be maintained. If the dealer sets the price too low then the supply will run out. In that case, not only will the dealer lose income (nothing left to sell) but also at the end of the season 'the hardships of a dearth [and] the dreadful horrors of famine' will be experienced.

Smith is well aware that those circumstances generate social unrest and that this has often prompted government intervention to oversee the distribution. He claims, on the contrary, that his argument by allowing the dealers to follow their own interests by adjusting their prices is the 'only effective' way to prevent 'the miseries of famine'. More pointedly, he declares that it is the 'violence of government' by attempting 'by improper means' to ease dearth that has caused famine. In short, the discrete decisions of individuals (in this case the price-setting by corn merchants) is a superior method of distributing goods, than some centralized and opportunistic political decision; a conclusion that goes a long way to explaining Smith's subsequent status as the flag-bearer of those who argue for the superiority of market economies to centrally planned ones.

In the case of corn the interests of the merchant and consumer align. Underlying this alignment, and the practical advantages of free trade, is a fundamental general principle. This principle is natural liberty.

Natural liberty

The term 'natural liberty' is not novel; it was an important component in political theorizing from the 16th century onwards. Smith, however, gives it a distinctive application. According to Smith's definition, the 'system of natural liberty' is when

> every man, as long as he does not violate the laws of justice is left
> perfectly free to pursue his own interest his own way and to bring
> both his industry and capital into competition with those of any
> other man or order of men.

It follows from this, and in stark contrast to mercantilist practice, that government is completely discharged from 'a duty...of superintending the industry of private people and of directing it towards the employments most suitable to the interest of society' (*WN* 687).

The doctrine of relieving the government from economic superintendence is frequently labelled 'laissez-faire' but although the term was current Smith never uses it. This restriction of the role of government avoids a further fault in mercantilism. Its policy of artificially steering the economy assumes humans (governments) possess enough wisdom or knowledge to ascertain what, and how much, direction is in fact in the interests of society. But for Smith they are deluding themselves. Nobody (and especially not governments) is that wise or knowledgeable.

Smith's confidence that government's role can be safely restricted lies in his conviction that everyone seeks to better their own condition. Given freedom and security this natural urge to self-identified betterment is, he claims, so powerful that, in spite of the extravagance of government and foolish restrictions, it is able to generate social wealth and prosperity. It prompts people to save and build up capital. This 'private frugality', either directly or indirectly by extending interest-bearing credit, increases productive labour, and stimulates economic growth and thus overall national wealth. In another flight of rhetoric Smith underlines the key role played by that urge by describing it as a desire that never leaves us from the womb to the grave. There is, he goes on, scarcely any time when individuals are so satisfied with their lot that they do not wish some improvement. They typically see increasing their 'fortune' as the means to this improvement. This is not reprehensible. In the *Moral Sentiments* he had noted that frugality was esteemed even when it was directed at the personal 'acquisition of fortune' (*TMS* 190).

In less rhetorical vein, individuals are continually exerting themselves to find the best outlet for their resources (capital). Free of external direction or artificial interventions, people will make their own decisions about their own interests. It is a basic Smithian principle that the law should trust folk to take care of their own interests. It is against the backdrop of that principle that Smith's one reference to the 'invisible hand' in the *Wealth of Nations* occurs. This reference is rather 'tucked away'; given its subsequent fame/notoriety, it certainly lacks textual prominence. Like the corn-dealer, each owner of capital seeks his or her own gain but, 'as in many other cases is led by an invisible hand to promote an end which was no part of his intention' (*WN* 456). This unintended end is the public interest (the steady supply of corn). Smith reiterates his distrust of politicians by observing that he has never known much good to stem from deliberately seeking to pursue the public interest.

However, not all operations of the invisible hand produce a benign outcome, like availability of corn. In his usual circumspect way, Smith even hedges this explicit evocation of the invisible hand with qualifications. He says carefully that it is not 'always the worse for the society' that the public interest is 'frequently' the unintended outcome of individuals pursuing their own interests.

Between the lines, this pursuit of self-interest can be to the detriment of society and will not always redound to society's benefit.

The duties and role of government

For Smith, government in a commercial society has three duties: protection from external foes, maintenance of public works, and an 'exact administration of justice'. Smith's view of justice in the *Wealth of Nations* is the same as that put forward in the *Moral Sentiments*. It is strict, rule-bound, and indispensable. This duty of government is similarly indispensable. It enforces adherence to the 'laws of justice' (the rule of law) that provide the security that enables individuals to pursue their own goals, to enjoy their natural liberty. This security is absolutely crucial; its presence makes it a safe or sane decision to invest and thus increase industry and stimulate improvement.

It is one of Smith's basic points that a successful economy does not exist in a vacuum but depends on a stable legal framework. This is not an article of faith on his part but one that the historical evidence bears out. The message from Book III was that it took the establishment of a regular administration of justice to enable commerce and manufacture to flourish. If this third duty of government was more extensive than the enforcement of contracts, the payment of debts, and rule-abidingness in general then it would inhibit prosperity. This seemingly limited task is Smith's default position. But he is not dogmatic and he is willing to allow exceptions.

Government can properly take a positive role, even when this appears to infringe natural liberty. Most often these infringements of liberty are for the sake of greater liberty. They remove obstacles and Smith identifies many such cases for action. He attacks the 'absurd' legal practice of primogeniture (the first born exclusively inherits) and entail (inheritance is predetermined—causing

87

Mrs Bennet in *Pride and Prejudice* to hope Elizabeth will marry Mr Collins to whom the Bennet Estate will pass). Both these practices restrict the market in land.

He is more forthright in his opposition to the English poor laws whereby each parish had the responsibility to support their own poor, with the additional authority to eject immigrant paupers. Smith judged that to eject someone who had committed no crime and had chosen where to live was 'an evident violation of natural liberty' (*WN* 157). By penalizing mobility, the effect of this law is to entrench poverty. Accordingly, Smith supported its repeal. The same applies to the statute of apprenticeships and the exclusive privileges of corporations and guilds because they too prevent workers from working where, and on what, they please. The argument here is that the government should withdraw from certain tasks. In effect the legislation should be repealed thus relieving government from the obligation to administer and go beyond its three duties.

Smith also identifies cases where the default can be over-ridden. These interventions generally make some sort of appeal to the 'national interest' and invoke, implicitly, government's first duty, its responsibility for defence. The Act of Navigation 'very properly' gives British shipping a monopoly of their own trade (*WN* 463). This differs from the monopoly granted to joint-stock companies. Here the monopoly is a reward for the risks and expense in establishing new trade with 'remote and barbarous' lands. But this monopoly is time-limited (like copyright). Not only is competition and free trade the way to raise the wealth of nations but these companies have a lamentable record of mismanagement as well as a self-interested desire to retain their monopolistic advantages.

In justifying proper government interventions, Smith gives the example of requiring fire walls to be built. These constructions prevent the spread of a blaze and that prevention is a justified infringement of the natural liberty of builders. In this same passage, Smith argues on the same principle that regulation of the issuing of notes by banks is proper; they should be in large denominations and be immediately payable on demand. In a related vein, he justifies a legal rate of interest in order that capital is put 'visibly' in the hands of those who will make more productive use of it. It can also be appropriate to deviate from the principles of free trade in order to encourage home industry. For example, when a domestically produced good is taxed then it is reasonable that the same good should incur a tax when imported. Smith is clear that this is not a mercantilist policy. It still leaves competition in place, what it does is level the playing field.

Public works, education, and the well-being of workers

In addition to its duty to maintain external and internal security, government's remaining duty is the provision of what he calls 'public works and institutions'. These are activities that although in the general interest are not in the direct interest of specific individuals. This is because profits cannot be earned from the provision of a good or service when the access to it can't be controlled. Smith supplies examples of what are now regarded as classic examples of such goods. Prominent among these are roads, bridges, and navigable canals. In addition to these infrastructural goods, Smith also includes the provision of public promenades, parks, and gardens. Particularly important is his promotion of education as a proper duty of government. His argument here in Book V requires him to revisit the division of labour.

The opulence produced by the division of labour was an unintended consequence but it had other less benign results. These affect those who perform 'a few simple operations'. Smith uses some of his most powerful language to depict these effects. The simplicity of the specific task repetitively undertaken by an operative (the pin-maker), means he has no opportunity to 'exert his understanding or to exercise his invention'. As a consequence he loses the 'habit of exertion' and with that loss becomes 'as stupid and ignorant as it is possible for a human creature to become'. The 'torpor of his mind' renders them unable to indulge in rational conversation and incapable of acting responsibly or prudently when it comes to everyday obligations and commitments. The uniformity of the pin-maker's life also 'corrupts the courage of his mind', that is to say, it instils cowardice, which involves a 'sort of mental mutilation, deformity and wretchedness'. In sum, the opulence induced by the dexterity of the pin-makers and the specificity of their task is bought at the cost of their 'intellectual, social and martial virtues' (*WN* 782).

This is what will happen to the 'labouring poor', who make up the bulk of the population in a 'civilized society'. The very power of Smith's language in these passages serves to prepare the ground for justifiable government intervention. This intervention is a realistic proposition because what will happen to the pin-makers is not, in fact, inevitable. Like the difference between the philosopher and the porter (which was the consequence not the source of the division of labour) it reflects the operation of 'moral causes' not physical necessity. Government can therefore exercise moral causation of its own; it can take some remedial steps. Education is the key remedy.

The remedy focuses on those affected. Smith's proposed remedy draws on Scottish practice, where public funds are used to establish a local parish school. In the schools envisaged by Smith, children will be taught for a fee that 'even a common labourer may afford' (*WN* 785). He is opposed to wholly public funding because that would encourage the teacher to neglect his or her duties. (This was a conclusion drawn from his experience at Oxford University, in contrast to Glasgow where students paid fees with the result that they got a superior education.) The public purse will pay the rest of the teacher's salary.

But Smith's prescriptions go further. He also recommends a curriculum. The essentials should be covered. This means imparting basic literacy plus elementary mathematics, instead of the 'little smattering of Latin' that is sometimes currently taught. Smith thinks this sufficient for the 'common people' who, unlike those of 'rank and fortune', do not have the time and financial resources to live economically independent lives (*WN* 784–5).

There will be an incentive to acquire these basics. Before setting up a trade or attaining membership of a corporation the 'public' will impose an examination, or period of probation, in these essentials. The same requirement will apply before being allowed to enter 'any liberal profession' or 'honourable office of trust or profit' (*WN* 786). Smith clearly sees this public facilitation of education as a precaution, because even a relatively educated populace is less likely to fall prey to superstition or succumb to disruptive demagoguery. This precautionary or prudential role should not be over-sold. Even without these external benefits, Smith still affirms the principle that it is a proper task of government to facilitate the education of the 'inferior ranks' (*WN* 788).

Education is the seemingly obvious remedy for the defective intellectual virtues. More indirectly it also addresses the social virtues since an educated workforce will be less torpid and thus more able to engage with the world around them. The state has another more direct, if still oblique, role to play in fostering the social virtues. It can permit 'publick diversions', such as drama, poetry, music, dancing, and the like. This permission is granted to those who would 'for their own interest' put on these diversions, always provided this was done 'without scandal or indecency' (*WN* 796). These diversions will help offset the 'unsocial morals' and lift the gloom and austerity of the 'little religious sects' to which the workers are prone to turn. Smith extends his endorsement of competition to this arena also. When there is a multitude of small sects they will find it beneficial to tolerate each other and, in this way, any disruptive tendency to zealotry will be reduced.

The solution to the lack of martial virtues is more problematic. This is because Smith rules out the practical viability of a citizen militia. In line with the principles of the division of labour, he thinks a professional standing army superior, especially since modern armaments make individual bravery less significant than discipline. The relative ineffectiveness of a conscripted militia in a commercial society would be compounded by this enforced service running up against the interests and inclinations of the people. But despite his strong language about the loss of martial virtue his remedial recommendations are vague.

He refers to the military exercises that the Greeks and Romans made the citizens perform and how these maintained their 'martial spirit' and intimates that an adaptation of such a system would be a superior remedy than a militia. He suggests that giving 'premiums and badges of distinction' to those who excelled would be an incentive. He had used this same suggestion, using the same terms, in the context of the parish schools to encourage performance. The best guess is that Smith thinks a similar system of government-backed public rewards would encourage participation in activities that would help counteract the decline of the martial spirit. Participants would be nudged not cajoled. Whether this really amounts to the government paying 'serious attention' to the problem that he likens to a contagious disease is questionable.

A professional army and other public servants need to be paid and money has to be found to underwrite the costs of education and other public goods. There are two major ways these expenses can be met—through taxation and through borrowing.

Tax

Smith identifies four 'maxims' of taxation. These have remained benchmarks. Taxes should be proportionate to the amount of revenue acquired. Second, tax should not be arbitrary, how much tax and when it is to be paid must be certain and not at the whim of the tax-gatherer. Third, tax should be convenient for the payer. Finally, the tax should be cost-effective, that is, it should not cost more to collect the tax than will be received, nor should it discourage business or induce smuggling. Smith believed implementing these maxims would not only collect revenue but do so justly.

All tax must be derived from the three different sources of income—wages, rent, and profit. Smith discusses them individually then proceeds to a treatment of taxes that apply to all three sources. Smith devotes least space to wages (income tax was not introduced until 1799 by William Pitt to offset the cost of the Napoleonic wars). Taxes on labour will tend either to increase unemployment or to raise wages, an increase that is ultimately passed on to the consumer. Neither outcome is desirable. In the analysis of taxable rent Smith distinguishes three sources. It can be levied on land, on the produce of the land, and on housing. With respect to the last of these Smith observes that the tax falls mainly on the rich, an inequality that he judges as not 'any thing very unreasonable' (*WN* 842). In blunter terms a little later he makes it clear that it is an 'inequality of the worst kind' if the tax falls more heavily on the poor than the rich (*WN* 846).

The analysis of tax upon profit concentrates on that earned as interest (profit as such is the 'compensation' for the risk and effort in employing stock and not subject to direct taxation). Smith observes that, while a tax on land is necessarily upon a fixed asset, taxable interest lacks that fixity. The stock-holder, he says, is 'properly a citizen of the world' who can always leave the country if the tax on interest is thought to be too burdensome (now known as 'capital flight') (*WN* 848). This difference had long been a major source of political debate though Smith largely side-steps it. Nonetheless with his disparagement of the political talents of landowners, together with his underlying argument for free trade as the foundation of the wealth of nations, it is clear he is no supporter of the inherent superiority of the landed interest.

Smith devotes most space to taxes not levied on the sources of income. Here he distinguishes between 'capitation' or poll taxes and those on consumables, but he concentrates on the latter because the former in practice are arbitrary. Consumption taxes can be levied either on necessities or on luxuries. Smith's treatment of the former is another benchmark, important not only in economics but also in social theory and social policy.

What is 'necessary' is not the same as a bare physical minimum. Smith's definition is:

> by necessaries I understand, not only commodities which are indispensably necessary for the support of life, but whatever the custom of the country renders it indecent for creditable people, even of the lowest order, to be without. (*WN* 869)

He gives a linen shirt as an example. This garment was unknown to the Greeks and Romans and they nonetheless lived comfortably but today a day-labourer would be 'ashamed' to appear in public without that garment, its absence is indicative of a 'disgraceful' degree of poverty. It is the 'established rules of decency' among the 'lowest ranks of people' that fixes what counts as 'necessary' (*WN* 870). From this it follows that what is experienced as a necessity is socially relative (different in California than in Bangladesh). Luxuries are simply a residual category and are similarly relative. Following Hume and contrary to a long-standing and still current opinion, Smith does not, on principle, condemn luxury as a corruption of virtue.

The policy implication is that consumption taxes should be levied on luxuries not on necessities. These will be paid by both rich and poor. Both, for example, pay a tax for consuming tobacco and alcohol. Such taxes on the poor induce them to be 'sober and industrious' and that is socially beneficial. Their ability to raise a family and instil good conduct is enhanced and this will, in turn, minimize the risk of social disorder. Smith says these taxes act 'as sumptuary laws' (*WN* 872). His wording here is careful because earlier in the book he had scornfully dismissed sumptuary laws. This legislation, which sought deliberately and explicitly to control the expenditure that different social classes could spend on clothes or food, was common to most societies in Europe and elsewhere. Smith denounces it as 'the highest impertinence and presumption' for 'kings and ministers' to restrain the expenses of private people (*WN* 346). Unlike the taxes on tobacco and ale, which are discretionary (you choose to buy a pint), these laws directly infringe natural liberty.

Taxation can also be levied to help defray some of the costs of public works. But some discrimination is appropriate. Bridges, for example, can be maintained via tolls. This charge to be paid by users will help ensure the bridge will be built where it is needed. This outcome could not be guaranteed if it was a decision made by public authorities using general tax revenues. Smith refers non-specifically to cases where a bridge or highway has been built in order simply to embellish the view from a neighbouring palace or to gratify the vanity of a minister. Moreover the toll can be proportionate to use. Heavy loads, because they cause more wear and tear on the bridge, should properly pay a higher toll than lighter loads. Similarly regardless of weight, a higher toll can be levied on luxury carriages than on those transporting necessities. As Smith sardonically puts it, 'the indolence and vanity of the rich' in this way contribute to the 'relief of the poor' by making the transportation of goods cheaper (*WN* 725).

When Smith was pulling his book together there was extensive debate on the taxation of the American colonies. Smith contributed to this. He was, though, chided by his contemporaries for delaying the publication of his book in order to participate in the debate and thus making the volume seem to one his correspondents 'too much like a publication for the present moment' (*Corr* 188). That is unfair to the extent that Smith discusses colonies more generally, including those established in the ancient world. This is the occasion for a remark often misattributed to Napoleon. It was Smith who said that to establish an empire to provide for customers is one fit for a nation of shopkeepers but not for a government influenced by shopkeepers.

In response to the American crisis, Smith saw advantages in granting the Americans independence. This would reduce a burden on the British taxpayer. It would also generate goodwill that would facilitate free trade to the advantage of everyone (apart from those merchants benefiting from the status quo). But Smith was under no illusions, he knew full well that his scheme of completely free trade was fated to be a 'Utopia' (*WN* 471). Not only is there no precedent for a nation voluntarily giving up some of its territory but also, here reflecting a recurring theme in his book, because it ran counter to the 'private interests of the governing party' (*WN* 617).

Recognizing this solution to be unrealistic he puts forward some more practical suggestions. The colonies, unless they defray the costs by taxing themselves, should pay to the central government taxes sufficient to cover the expenses of their own administration. They should also make a proportionate contribution to cover central expenses, including those incurred in time of war. To increase the acceptability of this scheme Smith advocates giving the Americans representation in the British parliament. Once again reflecting his unflattering view of politicians, Smith thinks this scheme would gratify the ambition of its leaders.

Debt

Governments can also raise money by borrowing. This presupposes a developed financial system. Money evolved as a more efficient or easier way to exchange different goods. Gold and silver because of their durability came to be widely accepted as the unit of exchange. But as commerce developed so did systems of finance. Paper money emerged out of arrangements between merchants and this in due course led to the establishment of banks. Smith judges this development positively. As he figuratively puts it, paper money converts dead into active stock thus increasing trade and industry.

Paper money is only treated as currency because it is believed to have value. But belief is nothing tangible, it needs to be given some substance or underwritten. Smith therefore counsels that this belief still needs to be secured in gold and silver. In a poetic flight of fancy lifted from Jonathan Swift, one of his favourite authors, commerce is more secure when it rests on 'the solid ground' of gold and silver rather than when it is 'suspended upon the Daedalian wings of paper money' (*WN* 321). In addition, to enable paper money to carry out its beneficial function there has to be confidence in banks as the issuing agents. This confidence can however be lost. This happened, with serious consequences, to the Ayr Bank in Scotland, an event to which Smith explicitly draws attention. The collapse of Lehmann Brothers and RBS in 2008 indicate that this issue has not gone away.

What a banking system facilitates is the issuing of credit—lending money to invest in new capital. But the government itself can borrow. The extent of government debt was contemporaneously a vexed question (Hume, for example, wrote a savage critique). Smith's analysis of government indebtedness provides another case where the unintended consequences of individual action do not work for the best.

Thanks to the security provided by the regular administration of justice, those with capital will have sufficient trust and confidence in the government to extend it credit. Their funds would be safe and they'll get a good deal because the government needing extra money to meet extraordinary expense (usually war) gave a good return. But this set a dangerous precedent. Because the government can now foresee a source of revenue it doesn't build up reserves. It effectively passes the buck to the next generation to pay the lenders back. However, that generation will adopt the same attitude; and so the debt grows. Smith then proceeds at some length to itemize the various devices by which the debt is funded.

Despite the ingenuity of these devices, bankruptcy, when the revenues are insufficient to pay off the interest, let alone the capital, on past loans, is the ultimate consequence. This, Smith notes, is often 'disguised' by manipulation of the value of the currency. However, this manipulation only aggravates the situation. By undermining the value of money it extends the 'calamity' to more innocent people (*WN* 932–3). He thinks it a vain hope to expect the public debt ever to be paid back. At best it can be reduced by increasing public revenues (such as a more equal land tax, increased excise duties, and a greater contribution from the colonies) and/or reducing public expenditure, such as removing the various distorting subsidies in order to reap the benefits of more productive trade and thus taxable wealth. To this day these options (borrow/increase taxes/reduce expenditure) are how governments have to meet their commitments.

In summary

The *Wealth of Nations* is a justly celebrated book in the history of economics or the study of how an economy works. It combines a comprehensive reach with a systematic analysis. Perhaps above all, the justification for Smith's renown lies in his Newtonian achievement of reducing complexity to simplicity. Economic behaviour and institutions are not random or chaotic but can be systematized and understood as the product of a few principles. In the way that the *Moral Sentiments* gives an account of how humans make moral decisions so the *Wealth of Nations* gives an account of how modern economies work. Both accounts rely on some universal principles identified in a 'science of human nature'.

In the *Wealth of Nations* pride of place among these principles goes to the self-interested hope of everyone to better their own condition. But, equally significantly, that hope embodies the moral principle that everyone is free. Slavery is not only an economically unproductive system it is also 'bad' (*LJ* 453). On the bases of self-interest and freedom Smith built his most characteristic economic doctrines. Free trade is the best way to stimulate economic growth and thus increase the wealth of nations; individuals are the best judges of their own interests; and the outcomes of particular exchanges redound unintentionally to the general benefit. In the last analysis what really counts is that human life is made better as the 'miserable poverty' of the savage nations, as depicted in his Introduction, is left behind, and the twin blessings of opulence and freedom are experienced.

Although Smith's foundational importance is now unquestioned that was not inevitable, his legacy was not straightforward.

Chapter 7
Legacy and reputation

An image of Adam Smith appears on a Bank of England £20 note. The very fact that Smith is represented, and in that context, is a legacy of sorts. But it is doubtful if most users of that note, even if they pay any attention to the image, will be any the wiser as to who he is. If Adam Smith is known at all, it is very likely in the context of the 'free-market economics' of Thatcherism and Reaganomics. For some, this is a commendation; for others, guilt by association. Beyond token name-dropping, matters become more complicated. There is 'Smith' the icon and 'Smith' the thinker. These are not disconnected but the reason why his thought has been culturally or ideologically co-opted is down to contemporary political arguments not intellectual impact. Thatcherism was a reaction to the prevalent politics in Britain and Reaganomics was a weapon in the Cold War. In both cases they thought the 'free market' and a non-interventionist government were the tools for the job. Adam Smith enters the picture as the thinker who originally forged those tools. As a consequence he was co-opted to provide intellectual credentials or pedigree. Despite the opportunistic character of this co-option it is not totally fanciful.

The *Wealth of Nations* today

Similar to other iconic thinkers, like (say) Karl Marx or Sigmund Freud, Smith's work is invoked more than it is read. This is also largely true of contemporary economics, the discipline with which Smith is, and always will be, indelibly associated. But the subject has changed dramatically. One marker of that change is its lack of interest in its own history. For example, the books on economics and microeconomics in this series mention Smith only once. One consequence of this change is that any attempt to view the *Wealth of Nations* through the lens of contemporary economic theory is of comparatively little value. The prevailing orthodoxy is heavily technical with sophisticated mathematical formulae working from a simplified and abstract 'model' of human rationality. Nowhere does Smith use statistics or other quantitative methods (he says at one point in the *Wealth of Nations* that he has 'no great faith in political arithmetic' (*WN* 534)) and his writings across their range, including the *Wealth of Nations*, provide a complex account of how humans behave.

Why then is Smith ritually referred to as the 'father of economics'? When this epithet was first applied is unclear but the sentiment is present in the late 19th century in the judgment of Alfred Marshall (the leading British economist of that era). According to Marshall, the *Wealth of Nations* was 'the greatest step that economics has ever taken' because it combined a breadth of knowledge alongside balanced judgment. Smith owes his attributed paternalistic status to the fact that his guiding principles remain foundational. This has to be at the level of 'principles' because, of course, the world of 1776 is very different from that of the 21st century.

These principles are few but fundamental. They include the commitment to 'natural liberty' where 'everyman' is 'left perfectly free to pursue his own interest his own way', with its corollary that the 'sovereign is completely discharged' from the 'duty of superintending the industry of private people', which is just as well since executing any such obligation is beyond any 'human wisdom or knowledge'. Also included in these fundamental principles is Smith's basic contention that the job of government is properly limited to the tasks of external defence, internal order, and the provision of 'public works', together with his judgment that the pursuit of their own interests by individuals will generally produce a superior outcome than one emanating from some pre-designed outcome. These principles are central to the 'free market model' that Thatcher and Reagan took up in pursuit of their own agendas. The intellectual ballast for this model was not directly provided by Smith but by economists associated with the 'New Right'.

Craig Smith has neatly divided Smith's legacy on the 'New Right' into three streams. The 'Chicago' represented by Milton Friedman, the 'Virginia' represented by James Buchanan, and the 'Austrian' represented by Friedrich Hayek. All three representatives received the Nobel Prize in Economics. Friedman's 'Smith' is the one who emphasizes natural liberty and the benefits that come from individuals being left to pursue their own interests, and he quotes the 'invisible hand' in support. Buchanan's 'Smith' is the thinker who was distrustful of government and who appreciated the need for a legal framework. Of the three Hayek is the one who not only knows most about Smith but also has been his most influential exponent. Hayek's 'Smith' is above all the philosopher of what Hayek calls 'classical liberalism'. His Smith recognized the limits of individual rationality, realized that social order comes about spontaneously, and thus provided the basis of all critiques of planned or managed economies. Hayek's most famous book, *The Road to Serfdom* (published in 1944), is the one above all others that reputedly supplied the intellectual basis for Thatcherism and Reaganomics. But, while this helps explain the popular image of Smith today, it is still partial or incomplete.

This is appreciated by some modern-day economists. Despite the apparent gulf between Smith's methods and assumptions and those adopted by mainstream contemporary economics, bridges across it do exist. Two in particular are worth a look, each also represented by a Nobel laureate in economics and who pays attention both to the *Moral Sentiments* and to the *Wealth of Nations*.

The first bridge is the growth of behavioural and experimental economics. Vernon Smith, one of its leading figures, has openly and fulsomely praised his namesake. This type of economics is less concerned with what in theory humans should as rational actors predictably do to achieve their goals (or, in the jargon, maximize their utility) than how they actually behave. In order to gauge behaviour, experimental economists devise a variety of scenarios or 'games'. The 'dictator game', for example, gives one player $10 as long as some of it is given to another player. According to the mainstream account, $1 would be offered and accepted, because $1 is better than none. However, when played that is not the result; a low offer is often spurned. It is in an attempt to explain that result that the interactions outlined in the *Moral Sentiments*, such as the desire for approval, have seemed pertinent.

The second bridge is built by Amartya Sen. He has written an introduction to a recent popular edition of the *Theory of Moral Sentiments*, and his own economic thinking criticizes what he sees as the narrowness of the prevalent orthodoxy, especially its account of rationality. As Sen interprets him, Smith's emphasis is on the imperfections of markets not their theoretical perfection derived from allowing the invisible hand to operate. More positively Sen detects in Smith a serious concern with the effects of poverty and deprivation, and sees Smith as a forerunner of his own 'capabilities' approach that focuses on the actual ability of people to make effective choices about how they want to live their lives.

But the fact that current distinguished economists differ over Smith's message is not novel. Ever since the *Wealth of Nations* was published it has been interpreted differently.

The history of the *Wealth of Nations*

The book was rapidly translated—it appeared in Danish, French (twice), and German (twice), all before Smith's death in 1790.

The initial reception in Scotland was enthusiastic. Hume, who read it shortly before his death, exclaimed his delight, and others reproduced Smith's arguments (including his 'trivial' example of pin-making and his worries about the effects on the pin-makers). Although, it is an exaggeration to claim that the *Wealth of Nations* made an immediate impact or that the book penetrated deeply into the reading public, there is no denying that Smithian principles did percolate into the political/policy sphere.

Prime minister William Pitt in a 1792 speech declared that it is only in the *Wealth of Nations* that an explanation has been given as to how capital will accumulate when not obstructed by some 'mistaken or mischievous policy'; and he continued to remark that it is Smith who has furnished the 'best solution to every question connected with the history of commerce or systems of political economy'.

But even then the divergence in his legacy was already evident. In contrast to Pitt's view, Samuel Whitbread cited Smith in parliament in 1795 in support of a bill for minimum wage legislation. Whitbread was not alone and Smith's work was rapidly taken up by other 'radicals'. Thomas Paine, for example, commended Smith's views on banks in an argument about the role of the Bank of North America. One effect of this adoption was that in the early 19th century Smith was criticized from the Right. A case point is the 19th-century dispute over the Corn Laws, which deliberately restricted imports of food and grain to keep grain prices high and thus favour domestic producers. Smith was quoted by those who wished to repeal these laws, while the repeal was resisted by the landed aristocrats. It was only much later in that century that he was criticized from the Left because he had by then become associated with the glorification of competition and self-interest. This has persisted. For example, the influential British historian, E. P. Thompson, in 1971, identified Smith as an exponent of the 'new political economy', whereby, in a nice phrase, the economy was 'disinfected of moral imperatives'.

Thompson is only one in a long line of critics following the lead of Karl Marx, who was Smith's most influential reader on the Left. Marx both praised and damned him. His evaluation depended on where Smith stood in the history of class conflict. Smith represents a bourgeoisie 'still struggling with the relics of feudal society'. As a representative of the rising and still revolutionary bourgeoisie, Smith could provide an insightful analysis of the old order. In this respect Marx could freely adopt and adapt a range of Smith's views, including the distinction between use and exchange value; the central importance of labour; along with the difference between its productive and unproductive forms. But for Marx, Smith's view is limited. He fails, above all, to acknowledge that his 'commercial society' is destined to be superseded by a new communist order. What Smith treats as unalterable facts about human nature, such as self-interest or competitiveness, are rather the transient products of a particular historical era. Once the bourgeoisie had gained its ascendancy (in about 1830) then, in Marx's view, Smith's 'economics' was used to justify the status quo. More particularly it was used to serve the interests of the ruling class and oppose those of the working class.

On the long view, Smith and Marx share one basic principle. They both think that labour is the key factor in explaining price and value. This is often labelled the 'classical' or objectivist view. In the late 19th century there was a fundamental shift to what Ludwig von Mises, one of its prime movers, called subjectivist economics. And here is the root of the so-called 'marginal revolution' that lies at the heart of the dominant orthodoxy.

The focus is on individual preferences not the process of production. In an often quoted remark, Lionel Robbins defined economics as 'the science which studies human behaviour as a relationship between ends and scarce means which have alternative uses'. The value of any good depends solely on a comparison with other goods. It is an expression of relative scarcity and price is the monetary expression of how much people are willing to pay.

There is nothing more. Gold, for example, is not 'valuable' because it is a particular metal or has required so much labour to extract, but because it is scarce relative to demand.

The relation between Marx and Smith throws up another aspect of the legacy of the *Wealth of Nations*. From its early translations the book was used to argue for (or against) particular policies in, among other places, Spain, Portugal, and Latin America. This same pattern has been repeated more recently in Japan and China. When Japan made the self-conscious decision to end a long period of isolation from the outside world and modernize (the 'Meiji Restoration' of 1868) Marx and Smith were the two obvious models, with both discussing the transition from a feudal to a capitalist or commercial society. Marx's model was initially more dominant and Smith tended to be read in the light of Marx's theory. But this changed, partly through the outlawing of the Communist Party and partly through the post-Second World War re-alignment toward 'the West'. On a scholarly front, this was complemented by an appreciation of Smith as the author also of *Moral Sentiments*. Japan has now become an important centre for the study of Smith (the University of Tokyo Library holds about half of Smith's own library).

In Japan, Marxism never succeeded in becoming the official ideology; in China it did. A Chinese translation of a version of the *Wealth of Nations* was published in 1901 but it was undertaken to push for internal reform rather than for pure scholarship (as was also the case earlier in Spain, for example). The real development of interest in Smith, as opposed to a Marxian gloss, had to wait until 1979 and the acknowledgement that the Marxist/Maoist model of social and economic development needed supplementing. Milton Friedman, for example, was translated in 1982. From this followed interest in Smith, so that there is now a flourishing body of academic work greatly aided by new and accurate translations. Smith himself said little about Japan (information was relatively sparse) but did make a number of comments on China. From the reports that he had read, he judged the Chinese economy to be stagnant. In line with his basic arguments, he recommended that it should open itself to foreign trade and that it needed to implement and ensure the rule of law.

The other Smith

Smith is more than an economist. He knew, thought about, and wrote on history, science, culture, as well as ethics. The legacy of the *Theory of Moral Sentiments* is far less eventful than the *Wealth of Nations*. However it was far from ignored when it first appeared. Across the Enlightenment it received a warm reception, with 18th-century translations into French and German. Although editions continued to appear periodically through the 19th century, its impact was muted. In Britain, neither of the two 19th-century mainstream philosophical approaches—Utilitarianism nor Idealism—paid it much attention.

Walter Bagehot, in a not unkind if rather patronizing essay of 1876, notes that the *Theory of Moral Sentiments* was once celebrated but is now judged to be of 'inconsiderable philosophical value' (though he also dubbed the *Wealth of Nations* an 'amusing book about old times'). A year earlier in his compendious *The Scottish Philosophy*, James McCosh, the president of Princeton, gave a reasonable overview of *The Theory of Moral Sentiments* but concluded it is more likely now to be read for its style rather than the theory it expounds. This judgment and others that were similar were echoed in other books.

One influential exception to this is H. T. Buckle. In his *History of Civilization in England* (1861), in the context of high praise of Smith's work as a whole, he floated the idea that the *Moral Sentiments* rested on sympathy, while the *Wealth of Nations* was based on the very different premise of selfishness. Buckle was popular in Germany and, as a part of that country's own internal debates, his book helped to fuel what became known as 'Das

Adam Smith Problem'. Was Smith's moral philosophy, as expressed in the *Moral Sentiments*, consistent with his economics in the *Wealth of Nations*? At stake was the acceptance of Buckle's dichotomy, whether the supposed sympathetic altruism of the *Moral Sentiments* was at odds with the supposed selfishness as the governing principle of the *Wealth of Nations*. Since it rested on misreadings of both the meaning of 'sympathy' and of 'self-love', this version has been thoroughly discredited.

The study of the *Moral Sentiments* received a fillip, thanks chiefly to the appearance of a scholarly edition in 1976 as part of the Glasgow edition of Smith's works. This matters to scholars but is hardly a development that in itself catapults Smith to wider attention. What it has done is spread the message that Smith's legacy is distorted if it represents him as the apostle of laissez-faire. A much more accurate picture of Smith's legacy is his contribution to liberalism.

Smith's liberalism

By linking Smith to liberalism more is at stake than his inspiration for the principles of the free market. That is too limited a perspective because Smith's thought is best appreciated 'as a whole'. For Smith 'economic' activity took place within society; the individuals who truck, barter, and exchange are already socialized beings. The key theme in the *Moral Sentiment* is that socialization was also necessarily a moralization. Thanks to parents, peers, and the general social environment, everyone learns how to 'fit in', how to behave acceptably. To engage in barter not only presupposes some form of communication but also some notion of fairness.

This means that for Smith economic activity does not occupy some 'ethics-free zone'. But he rejected a longstanding alternative version of a moralized economy. That account rested on a particular idea of the 'good life'. This idea relegated the role of economics. It made the moral judgment that a preoccupation with economic activity was less fulfilling than the truly or fully human activities of philosophy or politics. The place of 'the economy' was limited to 'means' (essentially staying alive, which animals and slaves do) not the 'ends' that make a human life worth living. This version of the good life treated as potentially degrading or inferior the pursuit of material pleasures, such as the desire for a linen shirt, fresh bread, or a comfortable home. And should these morally inferior economic means become valued in their own right then this was judged a corruption or transgression of moral standards. Smith rejected that whole argument but that does not mean that he morally 'disinfected' the economy.

Just as Smith has no qualms about butchers selling their meat on the basis of their own interest nor has he anything against bankers doing their proper business on the same basis. But it would be a mistake to see this as a separation of ethics from economics. Smith did think social well-being was best advanced by individuals making their own decisions, and he was thus opposed to central attempts to direct 'the market'. However, what he really opposes is the attempt to direct individuals' activities, their 'natural liberty' to pursue their own ends in their own way, always, of course, within the constraints of acting justly. This commitment to individual liberty is itself a 'moral' position. From that vantage point, the power of the state cannot, for example, rightly or justly enforce what jobs its citizens can or cannot do, or what clothes they can or cannot wear. Smith, the Professor of Moral Philosophy (as he identifies himself on the title page of the *Wealth of Nations*), never forsakes that perspective.

The same moral argument that endorses liberty at the same time justifies actions to regulate that liberty in order to enhance the general welfare. This is why Smith does not contradict himself by seeing a proper role for government regulation. In the light of the financial crisis of 2008, an apt example of this role is his willingness to impose restraints on banks. Smith's own moralized economics can throw further light on the crisis. The financiers became so wrapped up in their own projects that they became oblivious to the weakness of their assumptions, as they enthusiastically pursued ever more elaborate ways of parcelling up debt, superstitiously following mathematical formulae (which most seemingly couldn't understand) that supposedly underwrote them.

Just as the mirror in which the pin-makers see themselves reflects back to them their own narrow horizons so too does that of the financial elite. They lacked critical distance to enable the moral self-reflection that would have instilled a sense of responsibility. In these 'masters of the universe' (to use Tom Wolfe's satirical expression in his novel *Bonfire of the Vanities*) the human propensity always to over-value the chances of gain and under-value those of loss was given free rein. Smith says this propensity explains the success of lotteries; and what the bankers did, it might be said, was play a lottery with money they didn't have. Or, at the very least, their calculations of risk were misjudged due to their self-enclosed environment, which also included the supposed regulators and credit-rating agencies.

These elaborate financial manoeuvres are far-removed from anything Smith could have contemplated. But the underlying psychology and dynamics remain. His cool opinion of joint-stock companies bears this out. He judged that this now prevalent form of economic ownership had definite downsides. In particular, because the directors of these companies managed other people's money, and not their own, they tended to be negligent and exempted themselves from close scrutiny by the share-holders.

The fact that Smith never severs ethics from economics gives a distinct tone to his legacy for subsequent liberal thought. Liberalism is a mansion with many rooms. Smith's chamber has a commitment to equality. Everyone is equal under the law. This is consistent with the fact that some will inevitably be wealthier than others. But it is inconsistent with distinctions or privileges based on birth or inherited rank. He is committed to equal liberty and equal respect—to which the porter just as much as the professor is entitled. Everyone should be free to make their own way in the world. Public authorities should respect that freedom and not presume to steer that personal itinerary on the specious grounds that they know better.

For Smith, individual liberty is not the only principle or moral value. It is less valuable in its own right than for what it makes possible. This follows from his moral theory. Individuals are social beings. Unlike some other rooms in the house of liberalism, individuals in Smith's chamber are not separate beings whose behaviour can be understood independently of their social environment or who possess 'natural rights' outside a network of social obligations. For Smith what is valuable about liberty is that it makes possible the greater public good. This 'good' is not about perfection. Smith does not envisage a society within which all is sweetness and light. He is not in the business of drawing up a blueprint for a 'godly city' or a 'land of virtue and wisdom'. Smith's 'good' is more down to earth.

For him the true public good (the real wealth of nations) lies in the world of material well-being. Consumption is the purpose of production. To consume more and better goods is to enjoy opulence, which, as he said in his Glasgow classroom, is a blessing. This is most effectively obtained through humans acting on their own judgment of their interests. But these interests are not merely self-serving. As the opening sentence of the *Moral Sentiments* stated, humans 'as a principle of their nature' incorporate disinterestedly the well-being of others (*TMS* 9). And yet, as his work strived to establish, that is not to reject on moral grounds the role of the pursuit of one's own self-determined best interests.

The business of 'economics'—the organizing framework for the provision of the wherewithal for living—is of itself valuable. Carrying out that business is a worthwhile task. It matters that humans can live lives not dragged down by miserable poverty. It is a noble endeavour to lift humans from penury. The endeavour itself is set within a framework of moral values such as justice, humanity, probity, and law-abidingness. They, along with the desire for praise-worthiness, underwrite the actual operation of the rule of law; the bulwark of liberty. Liberty like opulence is a blessing.

It is in this conjunction of opulence and liberty that Smith's legacy lies.

References

Chapter 1: Life and times

Biographical

'Oxford teaching' *WN* 761.

'great applause' quoted in W. R. Scott, *Adam Smith as Student and Professor* (Glasgow: Jackson, 1937), p. 187.

Scotland

'one of the most stupendous works' quoted in the entry for the parish of the barony of Glasgow in *The Statistical Account of Scotland*, ed. J. Sinclair (Edinburgh, 1791–9).

'Ayr bank' *WN* 313–15.

The Enlightenment

P. Gay, *The Enlightenment* (London: Weidenfeld and Nicholson, 1966), p. 4.

'Rousseau's *Discourse*' *EPS* 250–4.

'Jean Calas' *TMS* 120.

J. Millar, *An Historical View of the English Government*, ed. M. Salber Phillips and D. Smith (Indianapolis: Liberty Press, 2006), p. 404.

Chapter 2: Communication and imagination

Language

'any or all trees' *CL* 205.

'Latin is an older language' *CL* 204.

'in a single word' *CL* 216.

'replace the genitive case in a declension' *CL* 220.

'reference to this work' *Life* 293.

Association

'polytheism in the *Moral Sentiments*' *TMS* 164.

'the world around them' *HA* 50.

'advantage from its discoveries' *HA* 51.

'whether a polyp was an animal' *HA* 38.

H. Thayer (ed.), *Newton's Philosophy of Nature: Selections from his Writings* (New York: Hafner, 1953) p. 3.

Chapter 3: Sympathetic spectators

Empiricism

T. Hobbes, *Leviathan*, ed. R. Tuck (Cambridge: Cambridge University Press, 1991), chs 6, 16, 17.

A. Cooper (3rd Lord) Shaftesbury, *Characteristics* (London: Grant Richards, 1900), 2 vols: I, p. 262.

B. Mandeville, *Fable of the Bees*, ed. F. Kaye (Indianapolis: Liberty Press 1988), 2 vols: I, pp. 51, 324.

Hutcheson

F. Hutcheson, *Philosophical Works*, ed. R. Downie (London: Everyman Library, 1994), pp. 71, 109, 135, 88, 99.

F. Hutcheson, *On the Passions and Affections* (London: 1728), p. 24.

Sympathy

D. Hume, *A Treatise of Human Nature*, ed. D. Norton (Oxford: Oxford University Press, 2002), p. 579.

F. Hutcheson, *Philosophical Works*, ed. R. Downie (London: Everyman Library, 1994), p. 199.

Impartial spectator

'punishment in another life' *TMS* 91.

Relativism

'merchants who want to restrict trade' *TMS* 54.

'mind-numbing work' *WN* 782.

Chapter 4: Living virtuously

'the sentiment of resentment' *TMS* 79.

Justice

'so severe a punishment' *TMS* 90.

Benevolence

'fellow-citizens' *TMS* 219.
'more expansive views or arguments' *TMS* 269.

Invisible hand

'invisible hand in *Astronomy*' *HA* 49.
'baubles and trinkets' *TMS* 181–3.

Ranks

'virtue and fortune happily coincide' *TMS* 55, 63.
'oppressive power of the aristocracy' *WN* 944.

Prudence

'diminishes their humanity' *TMS* 206.
'found to the highest degree' *TMS* 153.

Chapter 5: Making and working

'modern economic thinking' R. Thaler, *Misbehaving: The Making of Behavioral Economics* (Norton: New York, 2015), p. 7.

D. Hume, *Political Discourses* (1752), in E. Miller (ed.), *Essays: Moral, Political and Literary* (Indianapolis: Liberty Press, 1987).

R. Cantillon, *Essai sur la nature du commerce en général* (1755), trans. A. Murphy (Indianapolis: Liberty Press, 2015).

Stages

P. Lafitau, *Moeurs des Savages Ameriquains, comparées aux Moeurs des Premiers Temps* (Paris, 1724), 2 vols.

Tacitus, *Germania* (London: Loeb Library, 1914).

'four types of society' *LJ* 14–16.

The division of labour

'strongest of human desires' *TMS* 336.
'coarse woollen coat' *WN* 22–3.

Labour, price, and value

'sugar and so on' *WN* 38.
'commanding the labour' *WN* 65.

K. Marx, *Capital*, Vol. 1 (1857), ed. F. Engels (New York: International Publishers, 1967), p. 81n.

'most important in the whole book' *WN* 660.
'church, law and medicine' *WN* 331.

Rent

'example of kelp' *WN* 161.
'developed infrastructure' *WN* 163.

Social orders

'each order deficient' *WN* 265–6.

Chapter 6: Trading and spending

Mercantile politics

'core objective of mercantile system' *WN* 429, 452, 471.

Free trade

'cheaper claret' *WN* 458.
'attention paid to corn' *WN* 524–6.

Natural liberty

'womb to the grave' *WN* 341.
'distrust politicians' *WN* 456.
'bank regulations' *WN* 324.
'legal rate of interest' *WN* 357.
'import tax' *WN* 465.

Government

'restrict market in land' *WN* 384.
'on what they please' *WN* 152.

Public works

'roads etc.' *WN* 724.
'education proper duty' *WN* 824.
'Oxford university' *WN* 760.
'recommendations are vague' *WN* 698–9.
'is questionable' *WN* 786.

Tax

'four maxims' *WN* 825.
D. Hume, 'Of Refinement of Arts', in E. Miller (ed.), *Essays: Moral, Political and Literary* (Indianapolis: Liberty Press, 1987).
'nation of shopkeepers' *WN* 613.

'American representation' *WN* 617.
'ambition of its leaders' *WN* 624.

Debt

'dead into active stock' *LJ* 379, *WN* 321.
'Ayr bank' *WN* 313.
D. Hume, 'Of Public Credit', in E. Miller (ed.), *Essays: Moral, Political and Literary* (Indianapolis: Liberty Press, 1987).
'ingenuity of these devices' *WN* 911.
'opulence and freedom' *LJ* 185.

Chapter 7: Legacy and reputation

A. Marshall, *Principles of Economics* (London: Macmillan, 1890), p. 55.
C. Smith, 'Adam Smith and the New Right', in C. Berry, M. P. Paganelli, and C. Smith (eds), *The Oxford Handbook of Adam Smith* (Oxford: Oxford University Press, 2013) (with references to the writings of Friedman, Buchanan, and Hayek).
V. Smith, 'The Two Faces of Adam Smith', *Southern Economic Journal* 65 (1998) 1–19 (and several other publications).
A. Sen, 'Use and Abuses of Adam Smith', *History of Political Economy* 43 (2011) 257–71 (and several other publications).
S. Whitbread quoted in E. Rothschild, 'Adam Smith and Conservative Economics', *Economic History Review* 45 (1992) 74–96.
T. Paine quoted in J. Keane, *Tom Paine: A Political Life* (London: Bloomsbury, 1995), pp. 257–8.
E. P. Thompson, *Customs in Common* (London: Merlin Press, 1991), p. 201.
K. Marx, *Poverty of Philosophy* (London: Martin Lawrence, n.d.), p. 105.
L. von Mises, *Human Action* (London: Hodge, 1949), p. 3.
L. Robbins, *An Essay on the Nature and Significance of Economic Science*, 2nd edn (Macmillan: London, 1948), pp. 16, 55.
'China stagnant' *WN* 111–12.
'China open to trade' *WN* 89–90.
'China rule of law' *WN* 680.
W. Bagehot, 'Adam Smith as a Person', in N. St-J. Sevas (ed.), *Bagehot's Historical Essays* (Garden City, NY: Anchor Doubleday, 1965), pp. 91, 101.

J. McCosh, *The Scottish Philosophy* (London: Macmillan, 1875), p. 170.

H. T. Buckle, *History of Civilization in England*, 3 vols. (London: Grant Richards, 1861), vol. III, p. 314.

Liberalism

'the success of lotteries' *WN* 125.

'opinion of joint-stock companies' *WN* 641.

'consumption is the purpose of production' *WN* 660.

'opulence is a blessing' *LJ* 185.

Further reading

The best way initially to approach Smith is by consulting a collection of commentaries. These cover the full scope of his work.

C. J. Berry, M. P. Paganelli, and C. Smith (eds), *Oxford Handbook of Adam Smith* (Oxford: Oxford University Press, 2013 (paperback 2016)).

K. Haakonssen (ed.), *The Cambridge Companion to Adam Smith* (Cambridge: Cambridge University Press, 2006).

R. Hanley (ed.), *Adam Smith: His Life, Thought and Legacy* (Princeton: Princeton University Press, 2016).

For a survey of recent writing, see M. P. Paganelli, 'Recent Engagements with Adam Smith and the Scottish Enlightenment', *History of Political Economy*, vol. 47 (2015).

A. Skinner and T. Wilson (eds), *Essays on Adam Smith* (Oxford: Clarendon Press, 1975).

J. Young (ed.), *The Elgar Companion to Adam Smith* (Cheltenham: Edward Elgar, 2009).

Chapter 1: Life and times

Biographies

J. Buchan, *Adam Smith and the Pursuit of Perfect Liberty* (London: Profile Books, 2006) (US edition title, *The Authentic Adam Smith: His Life and Ideas* (New York: Norton, 2006)). A brief accessible introduction.

N. Phillipson, *Adam Smith: An Enlightened Life* (London: Allen Lane, 2010). A more specialized discussion that focuses on Smith's intellectual development and sources.

I. Ross, *The Life of Adam Smith* (2nd edn) (Oxford: Oxford University Press, 2010). A full-scale treatment.

Scottish Enlightenment

C. J. Berry, *The Social Theory of the Scottish Enlightenment* (Edinburgh: Edinburgh University Press, 1997 (paperback)). A comprehensive treatment that locates Smith's thought alongside his compatriots.

C. J. Berry, *The Idea of a Commercial Society in the Scottish Enlightenment* (Edinburgh: Edinburgh University Press, 2013 (paperback 2015)). A work that takes its cue from Smith but also discusses other thinkers.

A. Broadie, *The Scottish Enlightenment* (Edinburgh: Birlinn, 2001). A reliable, readable overview.

A. Broadie and C. Smith (eds), *The Cambridge Companion to the Scottish Enlightenment*, 2nd edn (Cambridge: Cambridge University Press, 2018). Covers all aspects.

For the general Scottish background

E. Foyster and C. Whately (eds), *A History of Everyday Life in Scotland, 1600–1800* (Edinburgh: Edinburgh University Press, 2010 (paperback)). Essays on general aspects of social history.

B. Lenman, *Enlightenment and Change* (Edinburgh: Edinburgh University Press, 2009 (paperback)). Focus on economic development.

C. Smout, *A History of the Scottish People, 1560–1830* (London: Collins, 1969). A social history now established as a classic account.

Chapter 2: Communication and imagination

On language

H. Aarsleff, 'The Tradition of Condillac', in H. Hymes (ed.), *Studies on the History of Linguistics* (Bloomington: Indiana University Press, 1974). The best overview of the 18th-century debate.

C. J. Berry, 'Smith's "Considerations"', *Journal of the History of Ideas* 35 (1974), reprinted in C. J. Berry *Essays on Hume, Smith and the Scottish Enlightenment* (Edinburgh: Edinburgh University Press, 2018). Offers a comparative view.

S. K. Land, 'Smith's "Considerations"', *Journal of the History of Ideas*
38 (1977). An analytical treatment of Smith's argument.

On science/astronomy

C. J. Berry, 'Smith and Science', in K. Haakonssen (ed.), *The Cambridge
Companion to Adam Smith*, reprinted in C. J. Berry, *Essays on
Hume, Smith and the Scottish Enlightenment* (Edinburgh:
Edinburgh University Press, 2018). Analyses HA and relates it to
Smith as a social scientist.

K. Kim, 'Adam Smith's "History of Astronomy" and View of Science',
Cambridge Journal of Economics 36 (2012). Explores the links
with Newton.

On rhetoric

S. McKenna, *Adam Smith: The Rhetoric of Propriety* (Albany: SUNY
Press, 2006). The only full-length treatment.

Chapter 3: Sympathetic spectators and
Chapter 4: Living virtuously

D. Raphael, *The Impartial Spectator* (Oxford: Oxford University Press,
1975 (paperback)). An accessible introduction by one of the editors
of the definitive edition of *TMS*.

More advanced works

T. Campbell, *Adam Smith's Science of Morals* (London: Allen Unwin,
1971). Sees *TMS* as an early exercise in social science.

F. Forman-Barzilai, *Adam Smith and the Circles of Sympathy*
(Cambridge: Cambridge University Press, 2010). Explores tensions
in Smith's ethics with references to recent debates.

C. Griswold, *Adam Smith and the Virtues of Enlightenment* (Cambridge:
Cambridge University Press, 1999 (paperback)). A philosophically
sophisticated work that provides careful detailed analysis.

R. Hanley, *Adam Smith and the Character of Virtue* (Cambridge:
Cambridge University Press, 2009). A focused analysis suitable
for readers with familiarity with moral philosophy.

P. Oslington (ed.), *Adam Smith as a Theologian* (London: Routledge,
2011). A series of essays that argue that Smith's thought is
underpinned by a commitment to religious belief.

J. Otteson, *Adam Smith's Marketplace of Life* (Cambridge: Cambridge
University Press, 2002 (paperback)). Draws systematic parallels
between *TMS* and *WN*.

Chapter 5: Making and working and
Chapter 6: Trading and spending

J. Evensky, *Adam Smith's 'Wealth of Nations'* (Cambridge: Cambridge University Press, 2015 (paperback)). A careful, accessible, systematic non-technical treatment.

G. Kennedy, *Adam Smith* (in the 'Great Thinkers in Economics' series) (Basingstoke: Palgrave, 2005). Clear overview.

More advanced discussions

T. Aspromourgos, *The Science of Wealth: Adam Smith and the Framing of Political Economy* (London: Routledge, 2009). Suitable for those with some prior knowledge of economics.

S. Fleischacker, *A Philosophical Companion to the 'Wealth of Nations'* (Princeton: Princeton University Press, 2004). Puts *WN* into a wider perspective.

S. Hollander, *The Economics of Adam Smith* (Toronto: Toronto University Press 1973). Thoroughgoing classical discussion.

Complementary works that range beyond the *Wealth of Nations*

M. Hill and W. Montag, *The Other Adam Smith* (Stanford: Stanford University Press, 2015 (paperback)). A deeply critical account but not an 'easy read'.

L. Montes, *Adam Smith in Context* (Basingstoke: Macmillan, 2004). Deals with selected topics, with an emphasis on sympathy.

D. Rasmussen, *The Problems and Promise of Commercial Society* (University Park: Pennsylvania Sate University Press, 2008 (paperback)). A systematic comparison of Smith and Rousseau.

E. Schliesser, *Adam Smith: Systematic Philosopher and Public Thinker* (Oxford: Oxford University Press, 2017). A wide-ranging account that brings out interconnections across the range of Smith's thought but most suitable for those with prior acquaintance with Smith's works.

A. Skinner, *A System of Social Science: Papers on Adam Smith* (Oxford: Oxford University Press, 1996). A collection of previously published works that covers many aspects of Smith by one of the editors of the definitive modern edition of *WN*.

C. Smith, *Adam Smith's Political Philosophy* (London: Routledge, 2006 (paperback)). Uses the idea of 'spontaneous order' as a motif and compares Smith's notion to later usages.

D. Winch, *Adam Smith's Politics* (Cambridge: Cambridge University Press, 1978 (paperback)). Focuses on Smith as an 18th-century thinker and is opposed to anachronistic accounts.

J. Young, *Economics as a Moral Science: The Political Economy of Adam Smith* (Cheltenham: Edward Elgar, 1997). Clearly written and argues for the unity of Smith's thought.

Chapter 7: Legacy and reputation

All histories of economics discuss Smith

R. Meek, *Smith, Marx and After* (London: Chapman & Hall, 1977). A collection of essays by the chief editor of the Glasgow edition of *LJ*.

M. Milgate and S. Stimson, *After Adam Smith: A Century of Transformation in Politics and Political Economy* (Princeton: Princeton University Press, 2009). Takes the view that economics took a wrong turn after Smith.

A. Sandmo, *Economics Evolving: A History of Economic Thought* (Princeton: Princeton University Press, 2011). Usefully and clearly discusses both predecessors and successors of Smith.

More generally

J. Hall, *Liberalism* (London: Paladin, 1987 (paperback)). A readable overview from the 18th century to the present day but in which Smith is a significant presence.

I. MacLean, *Adam Smith, Radical and Egalitarian: An Interpretation for the 21st Century* (Edinburgh: Edinburgh University Press, 2006). The title says it all.

J. Muller, *Adam Smith in His Time and Ours* (Princeton: Princeton University Press, 1993 (paperback)). Fluent account with observations on the legacy and its applicability.

Index

Adam Smith

Economics
A Very Short Introduction
Partha Dasgupta

Economics has the capacity to offer us deep insights into some of the most formidable problems of life, and offer solutions to them too. Combining a global approach with examples from everyday life, Partha Dasgupta describes the lives of two children who live very different lives in different parts of the world: in the Mid-West USA and in Ethiopia. He compares the obstacles facing them, and the processes that shape their lives, their families, and their futures. He shows how economics uncovers these processes, finds explanations for them, and how it forms policies and solutions.

> 'An excellent introduction . . . presents mathematical and statistical findings in straightforward prose.'
>
> **Financial Times**

GAME THEORY
A Very Short Introduction
Ken Binmore

Games are played everywhere: from economics to evolutionary biology, and from social interactions to online auctions. Game theory is about how to play such games in a rational way, and how to maximize their outcomes. Game theory has seen spectacular successes in evolutionary biology and economics, and is beginning to revolutionize other disciplines from psychology to political science. This *Very Short Introduction* shows how game theory can be understood without mathematical equations, and reveals that everything from how to play poker optimally to the sex ratio among bees can be understood by anyone willing to think seriously about the problem.

www.oup.com/vsi

KEYNES
A Very Short Introduction
Robert Skidelsky

John Maynard Keynes (1883–1946) is a central thinker of the twentieth century, not just an economic theorist and statesman, but also in economics, philosophy, politics, and culture. In this *Very Short Introduction* Lord Skidelsky, a renowned biographer of Keynes, explores his ethical and practical philosophy, his monetary thought, and provides an insight into his life and works. In the recent financial crisis Keynes's theories have become more timely than ever, and remain at the centre of political and economic discussion. With a look at his major works and his contribution to twentieth-century economic thought, Skidelsky considers Keynes's legacy on today's society.

www.oup.com/vsi

RISK
A Very Short Introduction
Baruch Fischhoff & John Kadvany

Risks are everywhere. They come from many sources, including crime, diseases, accidents, terror, climate change, finance, and intimacy. They arise from our own acts and they are imposed on us. In this *Very Short Introduction* Fischhoff and Kadvany draw on both the sciences and humanities to show what all risks have in common. Do we care about losing money, health, reputation, or peace of mind? How much do we care about things happening now or in the future? To ourselves or to others? All risks require thinking hard about what matters to us before we make decisions about them based on past experience, scientific knowledge, and future uncertainties.

www.oup.com/vsi